Reason and Revelation :

A Question from Duns Scotus

by

NATHANIEL MICKLEM

Principal of Mansfield College
Oxford

NELSON

1953

THOMAS NELSON AND SONS LTD
Parkside Works Edinburgh 9
3 Henrietta Street London WC2
312 Flinders Street Melbourne C1
5 Parker's Buildings Burg Street Cape Town

THOMAS NELSON AND SONS (CANADA) LTD
91–93 Wellington Street West Toronto 1

THOMAS NELSON AND SONS
19 East 47th Street New York 17

SOCIÉTÉ FRANÇAISE D'EDITIONS NELSON
25 rue Henri Barbusse Paris Vᵉ

———

First published 1953

Preface

THE following pages treat of the first question in the Prologue to Duns Scotus's *Opus Oxoniense* ; they are based upon lectures given in the University of Oxford under the terms of the Wilde Lectureship in Natural and Comparative Religion. These few lectures served as introduction to a more extended course upon the " Nature of religious Truth " ; they have been carefully revised, and various excuses or reasons may be offered for their publication. When a man has toiled for long and arduous hours over a small piece of work, he is naturally unwilling that it should all go up, as it were, in the steam of a single delivery and be dispersed for ever ; but there are better reasons than that. Duns Scotus, *doctor subtilissimus*, is one of the greatest of British theologians ; his chief work is named after the University of Oxford where he taught ; he was also, as his name, Duns, indicates, a Scot : yet he is one of the most neglected of theologians alike in Oxford and in Scotland ; neither the theologians nor the philosophers—least of all the philosophers in these days—are wont to study or expound him, and my attempt to bring to notice a few pages from his greatest work is an act of piety. Further, young theologians and philosophers who are not facile Latin scholars are woefully ill-provided with translations of texts from medieval philosophy, apart from the Dominican versions of St Thomas. I have thought that, beside the intrinsic interest of Duns's argument, students would profit from overhearing, as it were, one of the prolonged academic disputations that took place in days of the greatest intellectual excitement. Duns's discussion is relevant to our modern questionings, and it is profitable occasionally to consider how our questions are treated in a terminology, a method and a language very different from our own.

But my task has not been easy. This Prologue has

never been translated into English ; it is written in a style of considerable obscurity to those whose education has not been based upon the logic of Aristotle in its Latin form ; moreover, the argument winds in and out in the most labyrinthine fashion, and a bare and literal translation would in many places be intolerably difficult to follow and even unintelligible in modern English. While, therefore, I have kept close to my text and translated a very large part of it, I have reproduced much of the argument in paraphrase and have offered a few elucidatory comments on the way, as well as some little indication of the significance of the argument by way of epilogue. The numbers in the margin are references to the Quaracchi text, which I have almost always followed.

I have not been without help in my task. I was able to consult Professor H. H. Price of Oxford upon a number of obscure passages ; Professor C. C. J. Webb read and commented upon my typescript at an early stage ; Dr R. S. Franks most generously wrote me many notes ; and finally Professor T. M. Knox of St Andrews read my draft at very short notice, and has given me invaluable help. I fear that I am without excuse for the mistakes which I suspect I may have made ; my friends and helpers at least are guiltless. N. M.

Contents

v

Exposition

1.[1] The Prologue to the *Opus Oxoniense* treats of five related questions :

1 Whether it is necessary for man in this present life to receive some special doctrine by supernatural inspiration ;
2 Whether that supernatural doctrine which is necessary for man in this life has been sufficiently handed down in Holy Writ ;
3 Whether theology treats of God as its first subject ;
4 Whether theology is a practical science ;
5 Whether theology is called a practical science in itself in respect of the relation of action to an end.

Thus, in Duns's language, the first question is concerned with the efficient cause of revelation, the second with the formal cause, the third with the material cause, the fourth and fifth with the final cause.

We here are concerned with the first of these questions.

QUESTION I

2. " Posing the question we ask in the first place whether man in this life needs to receive by supernatural inspiration some special doctrine which he could not attain by the natural light of the intellect."

It was customary with the scholastics, once their question was posed, to set out first the chief arguments against the proposition implied in the question, these chief arguments to be refuted after the discussion of the whole question. Duns, therefore, first sets out the chief contrary arguments. **3.** The view that man in this present life does not need to receive by supernatural inspiration some

---

[1] The numerals in bold type reproduce the standard numbering of chapters in Duns's text, printed below, pp. 75 *sqq.*

1

doctrine unavailable by the natural light of the intellect might appear to hold for the following reasons.

3a. First, " every faculty that has for its primary natural object some common field is adequate to all that is contained in that field as its intrinsic natural object." For instance, sight is correlative to all things visible, hearing to all things audible. This is logically necessary, " for the field is by definition that which corresponds to the faculty. If there were a field in respect of which the natural powers of the faculty were inadequate, the field would not correspond with the faculty, but exceed it."

The argument to be refuted, then, is that, as the faculty of sight is potentially adequate to the whole field of the visible, so the intellect is potentially adequate to the whole field of the intelligible. Duns puts it thus : " the natural field of our intellect is ' being ' (or reality) as such. Therefore our intellect is a faculty adequate to the apprehension of any being whatsoever ; hence it is adequate to whatever is intelligible. It is adequate also to non-being, since, if we understand a proposition, we therein understand its negation." We know that " being " and " thing," or, as we should now more usually say, " reality," are the field of the faculty of intelligence, for they are " impressed upon the consciousness not by inference but immediately," since there is no other primary object which mediates " being " and " thing " to our intelligence. Hence, it is claimed, the syllogism stands : all faculties are adequate to their field ; the intellect is a faculty ; " being " and " thing " are its field ; *ergo* the intellect is adequate to " being " and " thing." The intellect means the natural intellect ; *ergo* man has no need of supernatural illumination.

3b. The second argument to prove that no supernatural illumination is needed by man is parallel to the first : " no supernatural aid is needed by the senses for the apprehension of their objects, therefore the intellect needs none." Of course, the intellect is not one of the senses, but the argument is not from senses but from faculties. It starts from Aristotle's proof in the third book of the *De anima* (432^b, 22) that " Nature never leaves out what is necessary." If this is true of lower and therefore more imperfect faculties, such as the senses, how much more will it be true of the higher faculties. If, then, " even in the case of inferior faculties nature supplies whatever they need to fulfil their purposes and achieve their ends, *a fortiori* nature supplies a superior faculty, the intellect, with all that it needs to fulfil its function and attain its end."

3c. The third argument to be met by the man who would maintain the necessity of supernatural teaching is thus put by Duns : " If any such supernaturally revealed doctrine be necessary, this must be because strictly within the limits of nature the faculty of the intellect is disproportionate to the object as thus knowable. It follows, therefore, that the faculty must be made proportionate to its object by means of something other than itself. This something other is either something natural or something supernatural. If it is something natural, the natural intellect with the natural addition will still be disproportionate to the primary object. If this additional something, on the other hand, is supernatural, the natural faculty is for that reason disproportionate to it. Hence, once again, it can only become proportionate to it by means of something else—and so *ad infinitum*. Since, then, as Aristotle shows in the *Metaphysics* (994^a, 1ff.), an infinite regress is impossible, we must abide by the original position that the faculty of the intellect is in itself proportionate to everything that is knowable and is adequate to every mode of the knowable."

This argument might be put simply in a modern dress : Truth, if we are to apprehend it, must be grasped by our intellect. To take an illustration, if the human eye is unable to see some distant star, it may be enabled to see the star by the help of a telescope ; or, if no existing telescope suffice, some further instrument may one day be available, for the star is potentially visible ; but no conceivable instrument could enable the eye to see a sound, for sight and sound belong to different worlds of discourse ; under no circumstances could the eye hear. But if, as some modern theologians have maintained, God is the completely Other, as different from the human as sound is from sight, there is no conceivable instrument or means whereby the mind could apprehend God. If, on the other hand, we do not assert that God is completely Other, there is no natural and intrinsic impediment to prevent the natural intellect from apprehending divine truth ; but, if the intellect can apprehend divine truth, we have no need of the hypothesis of supernatural revelation.

4. So much for the main arguments to be met. On the other side, says Duns, is the testimony of Scripture. " Every divinely inspired scripture," he quotes from 2 *Timothy* iii. 16, " is useful for teaching, for proof, for correction in righteousness, that the man of God be perfect. . . ." He compares *Baruch* iii. 31, where it is said of wisdom that " there is none that can know her ways, but he that apprehendeth all things knoweth her." He adds, " none can possess wisdom, therefore, except by means of him who knows all things. So much for the principle ; as regards the actual situation the writer adds, ' he granted her to Jacob his son and to Israel his beloved.' So far the old dispensation." The passage continues (here Duns cites the mistranslation of the Vulgate), " ' hereafter was he seen upon earth, and he had his conversation with men ' ; this refers to God's granting of wisdom under the new dispensation."

Thus the stage is set : on the one side is the philosophical argument that no supernatural revelation is necessary to man, his natural intelligence being sufficient of itself ; on the other side is the assertion of Scripture that supernatural revelation is necessary, and, further, that it has been given in the Old Testament and in the Incarnation.

4

Article I

The first article is an exposition of the opinion of the philosophers who hold that man in this present life needs no supernatural knowledge. **5.** " On this point," says Duns, " philosophers and theologians seem to be at odds. The philosophers hold the perfection of nature and deny that perfection is supernatural. The theologians, on the other hand, recognise the defect of nature and the necessity of grace and of supernatural perfections."

6. First the opinion of the philosophers must be adequately expounded. Duns puts it thus : " the philosopher, then, would say that man in this present life has no need of supernatural knowledge since he can acquire all the knowledge necessary to him by a consideration of the working of natural causes." The controversy, we might say, is between Aristotle and the Bible ; or, in more modern terms, between those who think that we need only scientific knowledge and those who hold that there are more things in heaven and earth than scientific thinking dreams of.

The philosophers, says Duns, rest upon a number of passages in Aristotle. **6a.** " First of all, attention is called to the passage in the second book of the *De anima* (430^a, 13–15), where Aristotle says that active intellect is what it is by virtue of making all things, possible intellect by virtue of becoming all things." There is no modern equivalent of these terms. According to Aristotle and the schoolmen there are two elements in an intellectual operation, one active, the other passive or potential or, to use the technical term, " possible." It is the part of the active intellect, ranging the universe of things knowable, to awaken or impregnate or " inform " the passive intellect. The active intellect does this by impressing the " form " upon the " possible " intellect. The passive or " possible " intellect is a capacity of understanding ; before it can operate, it must be " informed " by the " forms " of the real world which the active intellect—itself, like the passive

5

intellect, possessing no physical organ—derives from the images produced by the senses. It is a little as if we were to say that all thought involves perception and reflexion, though, of course, the active and " possible " intellects are not to be identified with perception and reflexion. The argument, then, is this : the functioning of the intellect depends entirely and solely upon the operation of the active intellect and the " possible " intellect ; when these two are brought into relation, and there is no impediment, their action inevitably follows. Moreover, " in respect of all intelligibles the active element is the active intellect, and the passive element the ' possible ' intellect ; these two faculties are innate in the soul, and there is no inevitable obstacle to prevent their operation. It follows, therefore, that in respect of whatever is intelligible the act of understanding is the result of the natural powers of these two faculties." This is somewhat as if in our modern terminology we were to argue that the mind always operates by perception and reflexion, that it has no other way of working, that this is a perfectly natural process, and that no place, therefore, is left for supernatural communications, since the mind is not constructed to receive them.

The argument is further confirmed along these lines : " there must be some natural active element corresponding to every natural passive capacity, for, if it were not so, nature would afford us a passive capacity that would be void and meaningless, since there would be nothing corresponding to it in nature to realise it in actuality. But," the argument continues, " the ' possible ' intellect is a passive faculty in nature with respect to all intelligibles whatsoever. This minor premiss stands to reason because the ' possible ' intellect naturally craves the knowledge of everything knowable ; by nature, too, it reaches its perfection by any and every cognition ; and it is, therefore, by nature receptive of every mode of intellectual activity." In other words, as the eye is designed for seeing all things that are visible, so our reason is designed for understanding the whole field of the rational, and there is no place for the supernatural.

6b. We come to a further confirmation of this argument in the sixth book of Aristotle's *Metaphysics* (1026^a, 18–19). Here Aristotle " divides theoretical science into metaphysics and physics (or natural science) and mathematics. In the light of the proof there offered it does not seem possible that there should be any further theoretical disciplines, since these sciences comprise the whole of the universe both in its entirety and in respect of its parts. Now, just as there could not be any theoretical science besides these three, so there could not be any practical science other than the practical sciences man has acquired, active and mechanical. Hence the practical sciences acquired by man are adequate for the full development of the practical reason, and the speculative sciences which he has acquired are adequate to the full development of the speculative reason."

6c. We come, then, to the third confirmatory argument from Aristotle. " He who has by nature the capacity to understand a principle has likewise by nature the power of knowing and understanding the conclusions involved in that principle." First, then, the major premiss : if we know first principles, we can by the light of nature draw from them all the conclusions involved in them. " This is proved thus : the knowledge of conclusions depends entirely upon the understanding of the original principle and upon the deduction of the conclusions from that principle. This clearly follows from the definition of knowing as given in the first book of the *Posterior Analytics* [1] ; but the deduction is self-evidencing, as is plain from the definition of the perfect syllogism given in the first book of the *Prior Analytics* (24^b, 22–6) as that which needs nothing other than what has been stated to make plain what necessarily follows. Where, then, principles are understood, and the deduction is self-evidencing, we have

---

[1] Has Duns in mind the implications of the discussion in chapters 2 and 3, or perhaps the end of BOOK II, 108^b, chapters 14–17?

all the prerequisites for the knowledge of the conclusion. The major premiss, therefore, is clear. But "—this is the minor premiss—" by the light of nature we do in fact understand first principles ; in these first principles all knowable conclusions to be drawn from them are implicit ; by the light of nature, therefore, we are enabled to know all those knowable conclusions."

The major premiss being that, if we know first principles, we can by the light of nature draw from them all the conclusions involved in them, the first part of the minor premiss is that we know first principles themselves by the light of nature. Thus " the terms of first principles are most general. These terms therefore we know by the light of nature according as we have the power of knowing or understanding by nature, for, as Aristotle says in the first book of the *Physics* (184ᵃ, 21–5), ' the things that are most general are those which we understand first ' ; they correspond to the door into the house. Now, as Aristotle says in the first book of the *Posterior Analytics*, ' we know principles in proportion as we know their terms ' ; hence we can know first principles by the light of nature."

The second part of the minor premiss is that all knowable conclusions to be drawn from these first principles are implicit in them. We prove it thus : " the terms of first principles are most general. When, therefore, they are distributed, they are distributed in respect of all subsidiary notions. Now such terms in the first principles have an universal application ; thus they cover all particular notions and consequently the major and minor terms of all special conclusions."

Thus on the basis of Aristotle's logic we have set forth the claim that scientific knowledge is all that man needs ; revelation is unnecessary.

Article II

7. In this second article Duns argues against this opinion of the philosophers. He offers three considerations.

First, then, " every rational agent requires a *clear* apprehension of its proper end." The major premiss of Duns's argument is that every rational agent must know the end at which it aims ; the minor premiss is in two parts : man is a rational agent, and man does not know his end ; therefore he needs supernatural revelation. Thus, " every agent acts teleologically by a desire for an end, while every *per se* agent (or rational agent) acts purposively ; every *per se* agent, therefore, seeks its end in its own way. Hence, just as a natural agent must have a desire for an end for the sake of which it must act, so the agent that acts through knowledge must necessarily have a desire for its end, which is the motive of its action and which is derived from knowledge. The major premiss, then, is clear." But, argues Duns, " a distinct knowledge of his end man cannot derive from nature ; it is necessary, therefore, that there be imparted to him some supernatural knowledge."

7a. The minor premiss that man does not by nature know his natural end is shown first from Aristotle, who, following natural reason, either places perfect felicity in the *acquisition* of the knowledge of separated substances, as he seems to say in the first and tenth books of the *Ethics*, or, if he does not definitely assert that such is the supreme perfection possible for us, at least does not prove any other supreme perfection by natural reason. " Thus, if a man leans upon natural reason alone, either he will be in error concerning his end except in the most general terms, or he will remain in doubt about it. Hence Aristotle's hesitating observation in the *Ethics* (I. 13) that ' if indeed there is any other gift of the gods to men, it is reasonable that felicity should be divinely given, and especially so in that it is the best of things human'." In other words, Aristotle, the supremely wise man, did not claim to know man's end by the light of the natural reason.

7b. A further consideration may be adduced in support of the same minor premiss. " We do not know the proper end of any substance," says Duns, " except by inference from its manifest activities which indicate that such and such an end is appropriate to such and such a nature. But we have neither inferential nor experimental knowledge of our human nature such as to assure us that *the vision of separated substances* is appropriate for us. *Clear* knowledge, therefore, of that end which is appropriate to our nature we cannot have." We might put the argument thus in modern terms : if we see a man running violently towards the station, we can infer that his end is to catch a train, for we can infer ends from actions ; but from the contemplation of history or from watching men as they live their ordinary lives, it is not possible to infer with assurance that the end of human life is fellowship with the angels or the vision of God : that is a matter of faith or revelation.

" This at least is sure," continues Duns, " that natural reason does not enable us *definitely* to prove certain *conditions of man's end* which render it more desirable and more fervently to be pursued. For, even if it be granted that natural reason should suffice to prove the bare fact of the vision and fruition of God as man's end, no proof would be offered that this end would be enjoyed under conditions of perpetuity and of bodily and spiritual perfection." Yet, he continues, " the perpetuity of this good is certainly a condition rendering man's end more desirable than if it were impermanent. Similarly the attainment of this good in a complete nature is, as St Augustine shows in his *De genesi ad litteram*, chapter 12, more desirable than its attainment in a disembodied state. The knowledge of these and similar conditions, then, is necessary for an effective pursuit of this end. Yet these conditions are beyond the reach of natural reason ; hence the need for the bestowal of a supernatural doctrine." This, then, is

Duns's first argument against the philosophers, namely, that every rational agent requires a *distinct* knowledge of his end.

8. His second argument is this : " every conscious agent in pursuit of an end requires a threefold knowledge : firstly, he must know *by what means and in what way* the end may be attained ; secondly, he must know *all* the things that are necessary to the end ; thirdly, he must know that all these things are actually *sufficient* for the achievement of the end in view."

" The first condition," he continues, " is obvious, since, should a man not know by what means his end is to be attained, he will not know how to put himself in the way of achieving it. The second follows from the consideration that, if a man does not know all things that are necessary for his end, he will be likely to miss it through ignorance of some particular thing that is necessary to it. As for the third, if he is not assured that these necessary things are sufficient for their purpose, he will not effectively prosecute that which is necessary, through hesitation as to whether he may not be ignorant of some other necessity."

But " these three types of knowledge exceed the reach of the natural reason in this present life." First of all, man cannot know by what means and in what manner he may attain his end, which is the vision of God ; for there are no means, there is no way, by which a man can of himself achieve his end. We cannot win or deserve eternal life. God gives this to whom he will. Duns puts it thus : " beatitude is vouchsafed as if it were a reward for merit to him whom God accepts as if the recipient were worthy of such a reward. Consequently blessedness is not the inevitable result of any of our activities ; it is God's gift, and it is given contingently, as God is pleased to accept some of our acts as leading to blessedness, as though it were a matter of desert. But obviously this is not something that can be known by the light of natural reason. Here the philosophers were in error when they averred

11 2

that all things that are from God immediately are from him necessarily."

As regards the other two types of knowledge, there is manifestly no certainty. We cannot know *all* the things necessary to our final end, for, as Duns says, " natural reason cannot give knowledge of acceptance by the divine will conceived as contingently accepting such and such acts as worthy of eternal life." Furthermore, " as for their sufficiency, that depends solely upon the divine will in matters where its operation is contingent." Thus is the second argument substantiated.

9. Duns has thus set out two arguments against the opinion of the philosophers. He now turns to consider objections against them. His first argument was that every rational agent must have a distinct knowledge of its end, and that man has no such distinct knowledge. The counter-argument falls under seven heads.

9a. First, " every created nature essentially depends upon some *per se* cause, and because of such dependence the *per se* cause itself can be known by a proof *a posteriori* from the knowledge of the thing caused ; therefore, since man's nature as being proportional to his cognitive faculty is naturally knowable to him, it follows that the knowledge of the end of that nature can be known by our natural powers from the knowledge of that nature." Duns's argument may be put thus : from our knowledge of the nature of anything we can know or deduce its end ; we do not know what a thrashing-machine is, for instance, if we do not know what purpose it serves, for the nature and end of a thrashing-machine are inseparable ; hence, if we have real knowledge of man's nature, we can infer the meaning of life and therefore the end of human nature ; now, it is argued, we do know human nature ; therefore by the light of natural reason we can deduce man's end, and there is here no need for supernatural doctrine.

9b. Secondly, if it be objected that, while in the case of some inferior nature it may be possible to deduce its end from the nature itself, this would not apply to more subtle and complicated natures, the answer is that in this regard the higher and lower natures are not to be distinguished, since the possibility of inferring the end from the nature is connected with the dependence of the created nature upon some *per se* cause, and the principle applies in both cases equally.

9c. Thirdly, it has been argued above [7b][1] against the philosophers that " we do not know the proper end of any substance except by inference from its manifest activities which indicate that such and such an end is appropriate to such and such a nature," that we have neither inferential nor experimental knowledge of human nature such as to assure us that the vision of separated substances is appropriate to us ; therefore we cannot have a clear knowledge of our end by the light of nature. The objection which Duns is now putting meets this argument by denying the premiss that we do not know the proper end of any substance except from its activities. On the contrary, it is here maintained that the proper end of a substance can be deduced from a knowledge of its nature.

9d. Fourthly, it might be argued that, though by natural reason we might be able to deduce man's natural end from his nature, we could not deduce his supernatural end. Man's natural end, presumably, would be such felicity as may be achieved through science, philosophy and virtue ; his supernatural end would be heaven or the vision of God. To this a reply may be offered by reference to St Augustine's saying (*De praedestinatione sanctorum*, I. 5), "So the possibility of having faith like the possibility of having charity belongs to human nature ; but the actual possession of faith like the actual possession of charity pertains to the grace vouchsafed to the faithful." We may say, therefore, that " if man by his natural powers can know his own nature, he will likewise be able by his natural powers to know the potentialities of his nature ; hence he will be able to know the potential disposition

---

[1] The numerals in square brackets are references to paragraphs in Duns's text, or to my exposition of it.

13

of his nature to that end to which faith and charity dispose him." If we know that a capacity for faith and charity belongs to human nature, we may argue that this capacity implies a supernatural object ; this, therefore, may be discovered without the help of supernatural revelation.

9e. Fifthly, " it is further argued against me," says Duns, " that man naturally aims at that end which I call supernatural. He must, then, be naturally disposed towards that end. Therefore, the nature so disposed being known, it must be possible to infer the end itself from the disposition towards it." Duns's argument might be illustrated in this way : if from a shoot pushing up from the ground we can infer that its end is to seek the sunlight and develop into a full-grown plant, so if we find that man is naturally a spiritual or religious creature feeling out towards that which is beyond nature, we can infer that his end is to seek and enjoy the vision of God. Therefore we can naturally know our supernatural end.

9f. Sixthly, we may come at the question from the proof offered by Avicenna in the third book of his *Metaphysics*, where he shows that " it may be known by the light of nature that the primary object of the intellect is ' being,' and it may be known by the light of nature that the idea of ' being ' is most perfectly realised in God." The argument then will be that " the end of any capacity is the best of those things which fall under its primary object, for therein alone is perfect rest and satisfaction to be found, as Aristotle shows in the tenth book of the *Ethics* (ch. 7). Hence it may be known by the light of nature that man in respect of his understanding is directed to God as his end." We might illustrate Duns's argument thus : if it belongs to the nature of an archaeologist to discover the beginnings of human life, he will be interested in neolithic remains, but he will be more interested in palaeolithic remains ; but he will only find perfect rest and satisfaction when he discovers Adam and Eve in the Garden of Eden : so on its intellectual side the urge of man's nature is to seek, beyond that which appears, that which really is ; now, ultimate reality is God himself ; therefore it belongs to man's nature to seek for God, and the vision of God is the end of man. This, then, we can infer by natural reason from the consideration of man's nature.

9g. Seventhly, the same point may be made in another way or from another aspect. Thus, " if by the light of nature man knows any capacity, he likewise knows by the light of nature the primary object of that capacity. It is further within his power to know wherein the idea of that primary object is most perfectly realised, for therein will be found the end of that capacity. Now the mind, as St Augustine shows in the *De Trinitate* (XIV. 4), is known to itself ; it knows, therefore, what is the mind's primary object ; it knows, too, that God is not excluded from the sphere of that primary object ; for, were it otherwise, God would be wholly unintelligible to the mind. The mind knows, therefore, that God is that ' best ' wherein the idea of the primary object is realised. Consequently it knows that God is the end of the capacity." We might put the argument in more modern terms in this form : if God were the wholly and completely Other, so that there were no analogy, no ratio, at all between God and man, the very idea of God would be impossible for man. But we have the idea of God ; therefore God is not excluded from the range of man's mind. As we know, the primary object of our intellect is to seek reality ; we are aware of God as the ultimate reality ; therefore we know by the light of nature that God is the end of that capacity to seek the truly real. We know therefore by the natural reason that man's true end is the vision of God.

These seven considerations, then, are all aimed at refuting Duns's first argument against the philosophers, namely, that man needs, and cannot have by the light of nature, a distinct or clear knowledge of his end. It has been urged in reply that, if a nature is known, as our nature is known to us, its end can be deduced from that nature.

10. We come now to objections which may be raised against Duns's second argument, which was that every rational agent needs a threefold knowledge in respect of its end, and that this threefold knowledge man cannot have by the light of nature [8]. It has been argued above by the objector that the end of a nature can be inferred from a knowledge of that nature itself. **10a.** Now in the syllogism there are two terms, the minor and the major ; one is known through the other, but the conclusion is reached through the middle term ; this middle term, then, must also be known and understood. Now we may prove by syllogism that B is the end of A. Therefore the middle term or terms of the syllogism or syllogisms must be known too. But the middle terms are the means whereby the end is, or becomes, the end of that nature. Therefore we must be able to know by natural reason how and in what way the end is to be reached together with all the things necessary to that end, and we must know that these means suffice for the end. We might illustrate Duns's argument by this syllogism : all plants that push up through the ground are seeking the sun : this shoot is pushing up through the ground : therefore this shoot is seeking the sun. The middle term here is " pushing up through the ground," and this is the means by which the plant seeks the sun. Hence, if we can infer from man's nature his end, we must make the inference through middle terms which are the means.

This argument is confirmed by a further consideration. When we know an end, we can infer the means that are necessary to it. " For instance, when we understand what health is as an end, we infer that such and such conditions are necessary to its attainment." We might offer a less ambiguous illustration : if we have to cross a river, and there is no bridge, we have to find the means by reflexion ; but the process of thought is that of deducing the means from the end to be attained. So, in the case before us, if we know that the vision of God is man's true end, we can infer the means necessary to that end from

16

the nature of the end itself. Therefore we can by natural reason infer the means necessary to the end, and Duns's argument that man cannot by nature have the threefold necessary knowledge fails.

11. These objections must be met. Duns, therefore, submits them now to criticism. Can the end really be deduced from the nature so that from our knowledge of man we can deduce his end ? Let us take the final cause, he says, together with that quotation from St Augustine [9d] where he says that " the possibility of having faith like the possibility of having charity belongs to human nature, but the actual possession of faith like the actual possession of charity pertains to the grace vouchsafed to the faithful " ; and let us take with them Avicenna's argument [9f] that we may know by the natural reason that the primary object of the intellect is " being," that the notion of " being " is most perfectly realised in God, that the end of any capacity is the best of those things which fall under its primary object, and hence that we may know by the natural reason that man in respect of his understanding is directed to God as his end. The error here, says Duns, lies in the supposition that this natural knowability of our nature applies to that particular and special element in it in respect of which it is capable of the consummation of grace, and in respect of which it has God for its most perfect object. " For our soul is known to us," he continues, " and our nature is known to us as such only in some general notion derived by abstraction from sensible things." A general notion of that kind, however, is insufficient in respect of the direction of our soul to such an end as we are here discussing, that is, in respect of its capacity to receive grace and thus have God for its object.

The argument might be set forth more simply for us in this way : Duns has to deal with the contention that, if we know the nature of a thing, we can deduce its final end, that we know the nature which is our own, and that we can therefore deduce from it our natural end without the need of revelation. He does not reject the principle that final causes can be deduced from the knowledge of natures, but he would prefer to put it in the form that, if we *perfectly* know a nature, we can deduce its final end. We do know our own nature up to a point—a disciple of St Augustine could say no less—but we do not know our nature in that aspect which would enable us to deduce its spiritual destiny from the nature. Though by the light of nature we may know that man is a spiritual being or even accept St Thomas's proof that he needs grace, yet we cannot infer from *man's* nature the promises of the Gospel (Duns might say rather, " the contingent will of God "), and therefore, since the Gospel is the mending or fulfilment of Creation, we cannot from our knowledge of man's nature infer that final end which depends upon the Gospel. This is not Duns's language, but it seems to be substantially his thought.

The objections to Duns's first argument have been set forth in seven paragraphs [9]. He now goes through them point by point.

Thus it was argued [9a] that, ends being deducible from natures that are known, " since man's nature as being proportional to his cognitive faculty is naturally known to him, it follows that the end of that nature can be known by our natural powers from the knowledge of that nature." In reply Duns says that this principle is only true in so far as the entity is known in respect to its nature in that particular aspect which determines its end. He means that we might have a very extensive knowledge of human nature, for instance, as human nature is known to biologists or psychologists or chemists, but that from *this* knowledge of human nature no particular final end could be deduced ; the data provided by the natural sciences, in fact, do not provide the metaphysician with the data from which final ends could be inferred.

Then, says Duns, " the minor premiss is false." The major premiss being that " from known natures final ends can be deduced," the minor is " human nature is a known nature." And as for the argument that man's cognitive faculty is proportional to his nature, " I admit," he says, " that the mind is identical with itself, but this does not mean that as such it is proportional to itself as an object except according to general notions which can be abstracted from possible objects of the imagination." Duns seems to be saying that the self cannot be known as objects are known ; the mind can know only what we call in Kantian language the phenomenal self ; it cannot know the noumenal self. About its noumenal self it can only make inferences from its imagining and sensible experience.

Duns turns to the second objection [9b]. It was there argued that if the end of some inferior entity could be inferred from a knowledge of its nature, which was assumed, the same principle would apply to human nature. Duns replies that even in the case of inferior substances their proper ends, that is, those proper to their essence, are not known as a matter of fact unless there are manifest activities of the substance from which the determination of that substance to such and such an end can be inferred. Duns means that, though the abstract principle be accepted that ends can be inferred from known natures, this only applies where natures are completely known ; we may often have genuine knowledge of a nature without having the particular knowledge of it which would enable us to infer its end.

The third objection [9c] had been a denial of Duns's premiss that the proper end of any substance can be deduced only from its activities. It was maintained, on the contrary, that the proper end of a substance can be deduced from its nature. It is now plain, says Duns, that there is no error in his proposition that the proper end of a substance is not known to us except through activities of that substance which are manifest to us ; for that proposition does not imply that there is no other means by which in logic an end can be known. No doubt, if a substance were really known in its proper essence, its final cause could be deduced *a posteriori* from the nature so known ; but as a matter of fact, in this present life, no substance is known to us in this way ; therefore in this present life there is no end proper to a substance within our mental grasp apart from such general and confused knowledge as we may deduce from the evident activities of the substance so known to us. It may be true, therefore, in principle that the end of any nature that is known may be deduced from that nature, and it may be true in principle that the end of any nature may be deduced from its activities if they are known ; but, in fact, in respect of human nature, we have not sufficient knowledge either of its essence or of its activities to be able to deduce from such knowledge its final end.

Duns turns to consider the fourth objection [9d]. Is it possible to infer not only man's natural end but also his supernatural end by natural reason ? The objector has said " Yes," basing himself upon St Augustine, who said that though the actual possession of faith like the actual possession of charity pertains to the grace vouchsafed to the faithful only, yet the possibility of having faith like the possibility of having charity belongs to human nature as such ; hence by the natural reason man may know the potential disposition of his nature to that end to which faith and charity actually dispose him ; therefore he heeds no supernatural instruction as to his true end. Duns meets this by going back to the point he made above [11 *sub init.*] that the mind is not proportionate to itself as an object except in respect of general notions which can be abstracted from objects of sense. All our natural knowledge is derived from the senses, or is in the form of images which are drawn from sensible experience. In respect of St Augustine's dictum, therefore, he argues that the possibility of having charity is a special relationship of loving ; it no doubt belongs to human nature, but it does not belong to human nature as an object of scientific knowledge ; we cannot deduce from sensible experience that man has a capacity to love God ; " hence this capacity is not knowable in respect of man by the light of nature, just as man himself is not an object of knowledge in respect of that whereby this capacity belongs to him." Thus Duns denies the minor premiss of the argument ; but he does not deny that God is the natural end of man in the sense that man is made for God ; this natural end, however, is also supernatural in the sense that it is neither to be known nor achieved in the ordinary course of nature but only supernaturally. We need supernatural doctrine to know our end and supernatural grace to attain it.

This line of argument is closely related to the fifth objection, which claimed [9e] that man aims naturally at a supernatural end, and that he must therefore be naturally disposed towards that end. " I grant that," says Duns.

The sixth objection [9f] requires longer consideration. We know by natural reason, said Avicenna, that the primary object of the intellect is " being," that the natural reason may know that the notion of " being " is most perfectly realised in God ; we may infer, therefore, that the natural reason tells us of our being directed to God as our end in respect of our understanding. To meet this Duns returns to the principle, which he shares with St Thomas Aquinas, that all natural knowledge is derived from sensible experience. " I answer the argument based on Avicenna," he says, " by denying its presupposition that by the light of nature we know ' being ' to be the primary object of our intellect, and that, too, without the recognition of any distinction in ' being ' as related to the objects of sense and the objects that are not of sense." Duns complains that Avicenna has here illegitimately imported the tenets of his Mohammedan theology into his philosophy. Avicenna " lays it down explicitly in the third book of his *Metaphysics* that the disembodied soul has knowledge of substance immaterial in itself ; he is bound, therefore, to posit that immaterial substance falls

under the primary object of the intellect. Not so Aristotle ;
according to Aristotle, on the contrary," says Duns, " the
primary object of our intellect appears to be the nature
(or quiddity) of the sensible object, and that, too, whether
the nature be sensible in itself or only sensible in its inferior
properties, that is, a nature apprehended by a process
of mental abstraction from sensible qualities."

The seventh objection [9g] was based on the
observation of St Augustine, who says in the *De Trinitate*
that the mind knows itself. It was argued, therefore, that
the mind in knowing itself knows what is its own primary
object, that God is not excluded from the sphere of that
primary object, and that, since God is known to be the
"best" wherein the notion of the primary object is realised,
the mind knows that God is the end of man's capacity
to apprehend " being." It is not easy for Duns to show
that his view is really consonant with St Augustine, who
went so far towards identifying theology with philosophy.
The explanation Duns offers here is that " St Augustine's
observation is to be understood of a first act of the intellect
which of itself is wholly adequate to elicit its second act ;
but in the case of ourselves in this present life there is an
impediment which prevents the second act from being
elicited by the first." He promises to treat of the matter
more fully later. It would appear that Duns understands
the " first act of the intellect " to be a sufficient principle
for producing knowledge of itself ; but the mind is
hindered from attaining this knowledge because it can
be moved to the attainment only by sense perception,
which is inadequate for this purpose.

But it might be said that man in his state of innocence,
or with his nature as it was first created, had the capacity
to know his own nature ; therefore, since ends can be
deduced from known natures, man could know the end
of his nature by deduction ; such knowledge, therefore,
is not supernatural. Duns replies that for the validity
of this argument man's knowledge in his state of innocence
would have to be determined, an obscure and much-

debated subject ; and, in any case, it is in respect of man under present conditions that knowledge of his end is said by Duns to be supernatural. " When I speak of ' natural,' " he says, " I mean natural to man in his fallen state."

Or again, it might be objected to Duns that, if he says that the primary object of the intellect is unknown because the intellect is itself unknown in that aspect which relates to an object of that kind, it might further be argued *ad absurdum* that no object is to be known as intelligible because our capacity is not known in that aspect which relates to anything as an intelligible object. Duns's point is obscurely put, but it seems to be this : if it be said, as Duns has said, that we do not know the primary object of the intellect because we do not know the intellect itself in that aspect of it which would enable us to know its primary object by deduction, the argument may be pressed much further ; it may be said that we do not know anything at all as intelligible because we do not know the intellect in respect of that faculty whereby things are intelligible to us. In reply Duns grants that we have not a knowledge of the soul or of any faculty of it so distinct as to afford us knowledge that there is any such intelligible object corresponding to it, " but from the act of which we have experience we infer the faculty and nature whose act it is to have respect to that as object which we perceive to be apprehended by that act. Thus the object of the faculty is not inferred from a knowledge of the faculty but from a knowledge of the activity of which we have experience. But of the supernatural object we cannot have either kind of knowledge ; in that case, therefore, either way of knowing the due end of that nature is excluded." That is to say, from the act of knowing something we infer alike the faculty of knowing and the soul of which it is the faculty. In this difficult passage Duns seems to be arguing that the objection which he is meeting rests upon a misunderstanding of the nature of knowing. For instance, we do not first know our capacity to be moved by music, and then from that capacity infer the existence of an orchestra ; rather, we become aware of the capacity by hearing and enjoying the music of the orchestra. We come to know the capacities of our souls, in fact, through the experiences of life which reveal them to us. Sense perception is the source of our knowledge of ourselves as well as of anything else in nature. Thus we cannot know the vision of God as the true end of our nature through any prior knowledge of our nature or through sensible experience ; such knowledge, therefore, must be supernaturally conveyed to us if we are to have it at all.

So ends, for the moment, the discussion of the objections brought against Duns's first principle : this was based on the syllogism that an end can be inferred from a known nature by the light of the natural reason, that our own nature is a known nature, and that therefore we can infer its end by the natural reason. **12.** Duns turns now to the argument against his second principle. He had argued [8] that " every conscious agent in pursuit of an end requires a threefold knowledge : firstly, he must know by what means and in what way the end may be obtained ; secondly, he must know all the things necessary to the end ; thirdly, he must know that all these things are actually sufficient for the achievement of the end." To this the objection was made [10a] that in the syllogism there are the minor and the major terms, the conclusion being reached by means of a middle term ; this middle term must be known and understood ; but the middle terms in the case before us are the means whereby the end is, or becomes, the end of that nature ; therefore we must be able to know by natural reason how and in what way the end is to be reached with all things necessary to that end, and we must know that these means suffice for the end. It is to this argument that Duns must now reply.

In principle, he says, he has already replied. The argument rests on an assumption that has already been denied, namely, that we know the end. But he looks for a moment at the confirmatory argument which was offered [10b]. " When we understand what health is as an end," it was said, " we infer that such and such conditions are necessary to its attainment ; therefore the same argument must hold good in respect of human nature." Duns replies that, when an end is known, and that end follows in the natural order from those things which are means to that end and naturally requires their prevenience, then, no doubt, the means to the end can be deduced from the end itself. But, he goes on, in the case before us, namely, man's true end, the end does not follow from the means in the natural order. The true end of man is the vision of God, but this is not to be achieved by any efforts of man ; man's end is only realised by grace ; " the divine will," says Duns, " is pleased to accept those merits as if they deserved that end and that reward."

13. So Duns proceeds to his third argument against the philosophers. Aristotle says in the sixth book of the *Metaphysics* (ch. 1) that the knowledge of unembodied substances is the highest type of knowledge, because it is concerned with the highest kind of being. Therefore, says Duns, " it would follow that a knowledge of that which is proper to such beings is both the highest type of knowledge and the most necessary, for as objects of possible knowledge those things which are proper to un-embodied substances are both nobler and more perfect than those which are associated with the things of the senses. But we cannot know these properties by our natural gifts alone."

Duns, then, invokes the authority of Aristotle against the philosophers. We may deem his argument somewhat sophistical, for to Aristotle the unembodied substances meant the unmoved movers of the heavenly bodies, whereas Duns understands by unembodied substances the angels. Aristotle states that the knowledge of spiritual (that is, of unembodied) substances is the highest type of knowledge. But, says Duns, the highest type of knowledge must be the most necessary ; this will be a knowledge of God and of the angelic world. It is idle to speak of knowledge of the unknowable ; Aristotle must, therefore, have meant that the knowledge of separated substances, of God and of the angels, as we might say, is possible. Yet, says Duns, a knowledge of the properties of God or of spiritual beings is not open to the natural reason. **13a.** For, if these properties were treated in any branch of knowledge open to our natural powers, it would be in the field of metaphysics, but we cannot have a metaphysic of the qualities proper to spiritual substances, as is manifest from two considerations that follow.

The first is this : the properties proper to unembodied substances " are not included implicitly in the primary subject of metaphysics, namely, ' being.' For this is what Aristotle says in the first book of the *Metaphysics* (ch. 2), ' the wise man should know all things as far as possible ' ; he means in respect of universals, not particulars. He adds, ' he who knows universals knows in a way all things that fall under universals ' ; he calls the wise man a metaphysician, as he proves in that passage that wisdom is metaphysic." Duns's argument seems to be this : Aristotle's view that the metaphysician has full knowledge of "being" in the abstract may be allowed, but not his view that to know the universal is to know the particular. Metaphysics deals with " being " ; but from the bare notion of " being " or from the abstract categories of " being " we cannot deduce the peculiar nature and qualities of any particular type of being.

13b. The second consideration to show that we cannot have a metaphysic of the qualities proper to unembodied substances is this : " such properties as those of unembodied substances," says Duns, " are not known by inference unless we already know the proper subjects of those properties, which subjects include the properties to be known by inference ; but the proper subjects are not knowable to us by the light of nature ; therefore we cannot by our natural powers know their properties." In other words, we cannot know the properties of God or of the angels unless we antecedently know God and the angels, and the knowledge of their nature would involve a knowledge of these properties ; but by the natural reason we do not know the nature of God or of the angels ; therefore we do not know their properties.

Moreover, these properties are also not known from their effects, for " the effects either leave the mind doubtful or lead it into error." Duns uses this illustration : we know as Christians that the First Substance, which is God, is intrinsically immaterial ; and we know that it is a property of that divine Nature to be communicable to three, that is, the Trinity. But arguing from effects, that is, from nature, we never could prove that property, because the effects do not proceed from the First Substance specifically as a Trinity. And, if we try to argue from the effects to the cause, the effects lead us all the more into error and the contrary of the truth, for in no effect do we find a nature numerically one except in a single individual. In other words, we never come across anything in nature which suggests that its cause is a threefold, not a single, Being ; nor is there anything in nature to suggest to us a Being that is Three in One and One in Three.

Further, it is a property of that divine Nature, in relation to things outside itself, to cause contingently. But its effects lead us further astray in the very opposite direction, as appears from the opinions of the philosophers who lay it down that what is First causes of necessity. This argument might be put thus in modern terms : Christians know that nature and history are in the hands and under the direction of God. On the other hand, the uniformity of nature is the fundamental axiom of scientific inquiry, and many philosophers have concluded that the world is a mechanical system showing the constant operation of necessary laws. It is impossible, therefore, to know God from a study of nature. Therefore man needs knowledge supernaturally conveyed to him.

Indeed, says Duns, the same argument applies to the properties of other substances also, for according to those philosophers their effects point rather to the perpetuity, eternity and necessity of these substances than to their contingency and continual newness. Likewise the philosophers appear to conclude from a study of motion that the number of those unembodied substances corresponds to the number of the celestial motions. So, too, they conclude that those substances are *naturally* blessed and impeccable. " All such ideas," he says, " are most absurd "—as indeed they may appear if with Duns we take the unembodied substances to be the angels. In fact, we cannot reason to the truth about God and to the vision of God as man's true end from a consideration of nature, or, to put it another way, from sensible experience. Therefore we need supernatural doctrine.

14. " Against that line of reasoning," says Duns, who always has contemporary philosophers in mind, " I argue and maintain that, whatever necessary truths about unembodied substances are known to us in our present life, whether they are known to us by faith or by special or general revelation, can be known by natural cognition." St Thomas Aquinas had taught that there are two different modes of cognition corresponding to the two different types of truth. Duns now argues that there is only one way of knowing, that is, by the natural reason with which we are endowed ; and whether the truth set before us be derived from logical deduction in the ordinary way, or be accepted by faith or specially revealed from heaven, it is by our natural reason that we apprehend it. Thus every truth can be set out in the form of a proposition ; and whatever the proposition, and whatever its source, it is by our natural reason that we grasp it. Duns puts it thus : " whenever by our natural powers we know the terms of any necessary truths of revelation, we are able to understand the truths by our natural powers ; now, we do by our natural powers understand the terms of all necessary truths of revelation ; therefore by our natural powers we can understand all these truths."

He first proves his major premiss, namely, that whenever by our natural powers we know the terms of any necessary truths of revelation, we are able to understand those truths by our natural powers. Such truths, he says, are either immediate or mediate. By a mediate truth he means one that is only grasped as the conclusion of a syllogism. " If the truths are immediate, they are, as Aristotle shows in the first book of the *Posterior Analytics*, known by means of the terms that are known. If the truths are mediate, then, since we can know the major and the minor terms, we can conceive the middle term between them, and then, by joining the middle term to the major and minor, grasp the premisses either immediately or mediately. If they are grasped immediately, then, as above, the proposition is understood, its terms being understood. If they are grasped mediately, we shall proceed by conceiving a middle term between the major and minor and by joining it with these terms, until we come to an immediate truth. Therefore we shall come at last to necessary, immediate truths, which we shall understand from the terms from which all the necessary mediate truths follow. By our natural reason, therefore, we shall be able to know those mediate truths through the immediate."

Duns then proceeds to prove the minor premiss, namely, that we do by our natural powers understand the terms of all necessary truths of revelation. The truths of revelation must be put in the form of propositions ; these propositions can be matters of discussion between believers and unbelievers ; in this case " the contention is not merely about names, but about concepts " ; that is to say, the unbeliever no less than the believer understands what the words mean, and therefore what the proposition means. " For instance," says Duns, " when a philosopher and a theologian dispute about the proposition ' God is both Three and One,' it is not merely the same phrase but the same concept that the one affirms and the other denies. Therefore every simple concept which the one has the other has also."

15. But Duns is not satisfied. To what has just been said he replies, " in regard to unembodied substances there are certain immediate truths. I admit, then, some such primary and immediate truth ; we will call it A. In this immediate truth are involved many mediate truths, that is, such as state in particular terms things common to the predicate concerning things common to the subject. We will call these mediate truths B and C. Now, no certitude supports these mediate truths except such as is derived from some immediate truth ; they are not of a nature to be known, therefore, except from that truth which is understood immediately. If, therefore, an intellect could immediately understand the terms B and C and mutually relate them, but could not understand the terms of A, and consequently could not understand A itself, to that intellect B and C will be propositions without significance." Such a man will be like one who can work out equations with x and y but does not know what x and y represent. " So it is in our own case," says Duns ; " we have certain concepts common to material and immaterial things ; these we apply to the one and the other in turn. But such intellectual constructions lack certitude unless it be derived from immediate truths which are concerned with those entities in their proper and special meaning ; but in this respect we do not conceive those entities ; therefore also we do not know those general truths concerned with general concepts."

To elucidate this difficult argument Duns employs an illustration which may have seemed lucid to the Oxford of his day but is not so clear to us. " If," he says, " anyone cannot conceive the notion of a triangle but can abstract the notion of figure from a quadrangle and conceive that, such a man cannot conceive priority as being the quality proper to a triangle, for it cannot be so conceived except as it is abstracted from a triangle ; yet such a man can abstract one priority from other priorities as in the case of numbers. The intellect which we are supposing could formulate the intellectual construction, ' some figure is primary,' because it can understand the terms ' figure ' and ' primacy ' ; but the proposition so formed will be without content, for it is a mediate proposition falling under the immediate proposition ' the triangle is the primary figure ' ; but this immediate proposition the man cannot understand because he cannot understand its terms ; he cannot, therefore, know that mediate proposition which only derives its certitude from this immediate proposition."

In other words, we may have the notions " figure " and " primacy " and realise in a general way that they must be related, but from the two notions we cannot derive the notion of a triangle ; our proposition, therefore, " some figure is primary " lacks content. In Duns's illustration the proposition " the triangle is the primary figure " corresponds to A, a first immediate truth ; the proposition " some figure is primary " corresponds to B. We might know something of the taste of a pineapple from descriptions, but we cannot know the taste itself ; we might be able to prove that there *are* unembodied intellectual substances, but *what* they are, what their knowing and willing is, we could not know without premises which only revelation could supply. There are many mediate propositions about unembodied substances, about God and the spiritual world ; we can discuss these with anyone because we can use terms that are applicable both to material and immaterial things. But these mediate or general truths have not the kind of certitude which belongs to the conclusion of a syllogism, unless it be derived from an immediate, self-evident truth. We can discuss with an unbeliever the proposition " God is Three in One " ; he will know in a sense what the words mean ; we can discuss the matter rationally, just as we can deal with x and y in the equation, but for the unbeliever at least such a discussion can never lead to the kind of certitude we need, because he does not know what " God " is except in some general way ; there is no immediate knowledge from which he can start. Such seems Duns's general meaning here.

Thus in the argument before us, says Duns, I deny the major premiss that a knowledge of the major and minor terms enables us to have a notion of the middle term. " In proof I say that those necessary truths (about unembodied substances) are not self-evident, but mediate ; and when you reply, ' then, when we can know the major and minor terms, we can have a notion of the middle between them,' I deny the conclusion ; for there are indeed occasions when the middle term between the major and the minor terms is *essentially related* to them ; it may represent the essential nature of the major or the minor term or be a quality, prior in respect of some derivative or later quality, of one of them ; through a middle term of that kind the major term may be proved of the minor in a universal sense. I am ready to grant, therefore, that whatever intellect can understand the major and minor terms can understand a middle term of that kind between such a major and minor ; for in a case of that kind the understanding of the middle term is involved in the understanding of the major or minor or is identical with one of them. But, on the other hand, if the middle term should be a *particular* that falls under the major or minor, and there is no *essential* relation between the middle term and the major or minor, then it is not the case that he who can conceive the major and minor which are general can conceive the middle term which is a particular in relation to the general major and minor." Thus, to revert to Duns's earlier illustration, a man may have a notion of figure in general and of primacy in general, but it is not the case that he must therefore be able to have the notion of triangle *in particular* ; triangle here is the middle term, falling under " figure," which is required for proving primacy in particular in the case of figure.

Duns's difficult argument here may perhaps be illustrated in this way : we may take the syllogism, all men are mortals ; all mortals die before they are a thousand years old ; therefore all men die before they are a thousand years old. Here the middle term is " mortals." If we really know and understand what man is, we shall understand the middle term because it is essentially related to men. Here, therefore, to use Duns's terminology, " where we can know the major and minor terms, we can conceive the middle term between them." But we may contrast a syllogism of another type such as : all Englishmen are shopkeepers ; Nelson is an Englishman ; therefore Nelson is a shopkeeper. Here the middle term is " Englishman." But we might know what a shopkeeper is, and who Nelson is, without knowing what an Englishman is, for not all shopkeepers are Englishmen, and unless we already know what an Englishman is, we cannot tell what of Nelson is Englishman and what is just Nelson. Some of the truths about spiritual beings which it is necessary for us to know, Duns means, are known mediately ; that is, they are not self-evident ; therefore, for the knowing of them we need middle terms, and these middle terms have to be given to us supernaturally because we cannot derive them by natural reason from the major and minor terms.

The third argument against the philosophers [13] was that, as Aristotle says, the knowledge of unembodied substances is the highest kind of knowledge, that the knowledge of the properties of unembodied substances is therefore the highest and most necessary for us, and that we, whose knowledge is derived from sensory experience, cannot by natural reason attain to this knowledge except in such matters as are common to embodied and unembodied substances. This argument, says Duns, is most conclusive in respect of the First Immaterial Substance, which is God, because the knowledge of this Beatific Object, if the term be allowed, is in the highest degree necessary to us. Now, by our natural powers we can only have a notion of God through some general notion that is common both to God and to sensible things. Or, if that be denied, we still have to say that the notion of God attainable in virtue of creaturely powers is imperfect ; the perfect notion is only attainable by virtue of God's essence. What was said above about the general and the special applies in another way to the perfect and the imperfect. The fundamental contention stands, that the knowledge of God is most necessary to us, that by natural reason we can have but a general notion of God, and that this falls short of our need ; hence we need the light of revelation.

16. The fourth argument against the position of the philosophers can be briefly stated : " that which is intended for an end towards which in itself it is indisposed must of necessity be gradually advanced to the right disposition in respect of that end. Now, man is intended for a supernatural end towards which in himself he is indisposed. Therefore he needs to be gradually disposed to the acquisition of that end. But this is achieved through some supernatural knowledge. Therefore man needs supernatural knowledge."

Duns has said that what is not in itself disposed towards its end " must of necessity be gradually " disposed thereto. But it might be said that a perfect agent, that is God, can without gradualness remove a defect and act without gradualness. Granted that absolute power could do this, says Duns, yet it is a thing more perfect that absolute power should grant man some co-operation or activity in respect of attaining his perfection than that absolute power should withhold this. Now, man can in some way co-operate in the attainment of his final perfection ; it is therefore a greater perfection that such a task should be granted him. But this is only possible on the pre-supposition of some imperfect knowledge preceding that perfect knowledge to which he is directed as his ultimate end.

17. The fifth argument which Duns adduces against

34

the philosophers he puts thus : " any agent that in acting uses an instrument cannot by means of that instrument realise any purpose which exceeds the nature of that instrument. Now, the light of the active intellect is the instrument which the soul in this present life uses when it understands by its natural powers. Therefore it cannot by that light achieve any purpose exceeding that light. But that light is itself limited to the knowledge to be had by way of the senses. Yet in this life we need to know many other things which cannot be known through sensible experience. Therefore we have need of super-natural knowledge."

But this argument, says Duns, seems to turn round upon its user. We can only apprehend truth by our reason, for we have no other possible organ. If our intellectual powers are only capable of dealing with material provided by the senses, they are incapable of dealing with truth that is not given through sensible experience, and therefore the argument that is intended to show that we need supernatural truth proves incident-ally that we are incapable of apprehending any such truth. This is how Duns puts it : " According to this line of thought the uncreated light will not be able to use the active intellect as its instrument for the knowledge of any pure truth ; for such knowledge, according to the user of this argument, is not to be had by way of the senses apart from special illumination. Thus it follows that in knowing pure truth the light of the active intellect cannot participate. This seems an awkward conclusion, for the attainment of pure truth is more perfect than any common act of the intellect ; hence that which is more perfect in the soul, in so far as that soul in intellective, ought to have some share in the achieving of that purpose."

Upon these last two arguments, four and five, Duns lays little stress. They do not seem very effective, he says. The fourth argument that man must gradually be disposed to that end toward which he is indisposed—and this must be through supernatural knowledge—would only be effective if it were to have been shown that it is to supernatural knowledge that man is directed as his final end, and concomitantly that natural knowledge does not adequately put man in a position to attain supernatural knowledge. The fifth argument, from the instrument, rests upon two presuppositions, the first being that man needs certain knowledge which is unattainable by way of sensible experience, and the second that the light of the active intellect is limited to knowledge through the senses. He concludes, therefore, that the three earlier arguments would seem to carry greater weight.

Article III

18. We come back, then, to our original question, whether it is necessary for man in this present life that he receive some special doctrine by revelation—to which, that is to say, he could not attain by the natural light of the intellect.

First of all we must be clear what in this connexion we mean by " supernatural." Any capacity to receive is correlative both to the actuality received, and, in another way, to the agent from which it receives. In respect of the actuality received, says Duns, " the capacity itself is natural or against nature or neutral. It is called natural if it is naturally disposed to the form that it receives, against nature if the form it receives be contrary to the natural disposition of the capacity, and neutral if the capacity be disposed neither to the form nor to its opposite. But in this correlation there is no element of the supernatural." An instance of a capacity against nature is that capacity of a stone to fly upwards if it is thrown. " When," Duns continues, " we turn to the relation of that which receives the form to the agent from whom it receives it, we have the natural when that which receives is related to an agent such as was intended by nature to impress such a form upon such a subject ; and we have the supernatural when that which receives is related to an agent that is not naturally given to impress that form upon that subject."

Duns's distinction might be put into modern terms in this way : the eye, let us say, is naturally disposed to see the colours of the countryside ; it is not naturally disposed to gaze upon the sun, and we can imagine that the eye by scientific devices might be enabled to see colours that are not normally visible. But whether the eye sees colours that it is naturally disposed to see, or colours that it cannot normally see, as long as we remain within the sphere of colour, no question of the supernatural arises. Now, I may see a red ball because a child shows it to me or because an angel shows it to me. If the angel shows it to me, the event is supernatural. Here there is nothing supernatural about the form impressed upon my consciousness, the form of the red ball ; the event is supernatural in respect of the agent, the angel. Now, when we ask whether man in this mortal life needs supernatural knowledge, do we mean propositions that are beyond the range of the natural reason, or do we mean propositions which are vouchsafed to us by a supernatural agent ?

19. " In regard to the question before us," says Duns, "when we have in mind the relation between the 'possible' (or passive) intellect and the knowledge actually realised in it, none of its knowledge is supernatural ; for any kind of knowledge is a perfection of the ' possible ' intellect in a natural way, and the ' possible ' intellect is disposed to any kind of knowledge in a natural way. But when, in the second case, we have regard to the ' possible ' intellect and the agent, here we have a knowledge which is supernatural because it is derived from some agent which was not intended by nature to move the ' possible ' intellect to that kind of knowledge in a natural way. According to Aristotle (*De anima* III), the ' possible ' intellect is intended by nature to be moved to knowledge by the active intellect and imagination. Natural knowledge is only such as is derived from the active intellect and imagination."

It is in virtue of the active intellect and the imagination, Duns continues, that all incomplex knowledge

37

attainable by man in his mortal state is to be had according to the normal rule. The term " incomplex " here may need some explanation. The old illustration of the " incomplex " is the Latin word *homo*, a man. Here " ho " means nothing by itself, and " mo " means nothing by itself ; only *homo* as an undivided whole is significant. But if we make the sentence *homo stat*, the man is standing, here *homo* corresponds, as it were, to " ho," and *stat* to " mo " ; but in this case each of the two parts has a meaning by itself ; the meaning of the whole lies in the relation between *homo* and *stat*. This, then, is an instance of the " complex." Now, in the case of incomplex things, says Duns, God can cause knowledge of them through special revelation, as, for instance, in a state of rapture ; but in the ordinary way such supernatural bestowal of knowledge, though possible, cannot be called necessary. But in complex truths the case is very different ; for even if we grant the full action of the active intellect and the imagination, many complex truths will remain unknown to us, even though the knowledge of them is necessary to us. Duns would say, that we have no incomplex knowledge of God, but we know by revelation that there is a Being, God, who is Three in One. The knowledge of such truths, then, must of necessity be given to us supernaturally, for no one has proved able to acquire the knowledge of them naturally and to hand it on to others in his teaching, since, so far as natural powers are concerned, these truths will be " neutral " for one and every man.

We may conclude, then, that when we speak of " supernatural truths " we mean such as cannot be derived from sensible experience but must be imparted to us by a source beyond this present world.

20. In a difficult section Duns then turns to the question of revelation. The original bestowal of such truths as these, he says, is called revelation. It is supernatural because its source is an agent that is not the agent designed by nature to move our intellect. It might be called supernatural in another sense, too : not, indeed, in the sense that the words are supernatural or that they cannot be grasped by the natural reason, but in the sense that they represent a supernatural object. Yet the supernatural object is not known to us immediately but through the agent that represents it. Duns says : " an object that in itself should cause the knowledge of such a truth as that God is triune, or the like, is an essence known in its proper nature ; but the essence itself knowable in this respect is for us a *supernatural* object. Whatever agent, therefore, causes the knowledge of some truths which are intended to be evident through such an object so known, that agent represents that object. Now, if the agent itself were to cause such a perfect knowledge of those truths as the object itself would cause if known in itself, then the agent would perfectly represent that object ; but if the agent does not cause such a perfect knowledge as the object itself would cause, then the agent represents the object imperfectly in proportion as the imperfect knowledge which it causes is virtually contained in that perfect knowledge of which the object known in itself would be the cause. So, in the case before us, the agent revealing the truth, God is triune, causes in the intellect some knowledge of this truth, but an obscure knowledge, because it does not cause knowledge of the object known in its proper nature. If that object were known, it would be adapted to cause a perfect and clear knowledge of that truth. Therefore in proportion as this obscure knowledge is included in that clear knowledge in an eminent degree, as the imperfect in the perfect, even so that which reveals and causes that obscure knowledge represents the object which is causative of the clear knowledge—more particularly because it could not cause the knowledge of any truth except as representing some object, nor could it as representing any inferior object that naturally moves our intellect cause the knowledge of such truths concerning the object we have in mind ; for, indeed, no such inferior object virtually includes any knowledge of those truths

—no, not even an obscure knowledge ; hence in causing even that obscure knowledge it must somehow represent a supernatural object."

We, might, perhaps, briefly express the main drift of the argument thus : the truths of revelation are apprehended by the natural reason ; that is to say, the truth that God is triune is intelligible alike to the believer and the unbeliever by the light of the natural reason. But this proposition is a supernatural revelation for two reasons, one because it is given to us, not through logical argument from the world of sense but by a supernatural agent, the other because the Object with which the proposition is concerned is a supernatual Object. Of that divine Object, in this case the nature of God, we have not direct knowledge. Our knowledge is mediated to us through the agent that thus represents the Object to us ; nor is this revelation perfect ; that is to say, we do not know the Object through the revelation of the agent as we should know the Object if we could know it as it is in itself. Our knowledge of the Object, then, is obscure, but it is, so far as it goes, real knowledge, and it is such as could not be derived from sensible experience.

Duns continues : " the difference between those two modes of positing the *supernatural* nature of revealed knowledge is plain when we separate one from the other. Thus, if a supernatural agent were to cause the knowledge of a natural object, as, for instance, if the supernatural agent infused into somebody a knowledge of geometry, that would be supernatural knowledge in the first sense, not in the second. But if the supernatural agent were to infuse a knowledge of the proposition, God is triune, or the like, this would be supernatural knowledge in both senses, because the second carries the first with it, but not *vice versa*. Where knowledge is supernatural in the first sense only, there is no necessity that there be supernatural knowledge of this truth, for the knowledge could be had naturally ; but in the second case it is necessary that the knowledge be given supernaturally, since it is not to be had naturally."

Article IV

21. In the fourth article we find confirmation of the three principal arguments of article two. Confirmation in this connexion means confirmation by authority. As Aristotle is the supreme authority for the philosopher, so is St Augustine for the theologian.

21a. The first argument [7] was to the effect that " every rational agent requires a *distinct* knowledge of its end." This is confirmed by St Augustine, where he says towards the end of the forty-first chapter of the eighteenth book of the *De civitate Dei* that " the philosophers being ignorant of the end to which those things should be referred were able to see something true amid the false things which they said." In the passage to which Duns here refers St Augustine enumerates, among the truths which some of the pagan philosophers were enabled to see, Creation, Providence, the excellence of the virtues, the love of country, the fidelity of friendship, good works, and all things that pertain to good habits ; what they could not see was the end to which all these truths pointed, nor how they were related to that end. Natural philosophy, we might say, is not blind ; it takes us some part of the way ; but it cannot tell us that man is made for the vision of God, and it is this that we need to know.

21b. The second argument against the philosophers [8] was that man needs a threefold knowledge in respect of his end, namely, how it is to be attained, all the things necessary for its attainment, and an assurance that all these things *suffice*. This argument also, says Duns, is confirmed by St Augustine, where he says, in the second chapter of the eleventh book of the *De civitate Dei*, " what advantage is it to know whither one should go, if one is ignorant of the way by which one must get thither ? " It is here, says Duns, that the philosophers were in error ;

for though they taught some truths about the virtues, yet they mixed falsehood therewith—as, indeed, St Augustine states in the passage quoted above, and as their writings make evident. Thus Aristotle in the second book of his *Politics* inveighs against the political theories set forth by many others ; but even his own theory is not above reproach, as when in the twelfth book he teaches that the pagan gods are to be worshipped. Again, in chapter five of the same book he says, " the law lays it down that no orphan should be reared." Further, in chapter eight he asserts that there are occasions when abortion is proper.

21c. The third argument [13] started from Aristotle's proposition that knowledge of the unembodied substances is the highest form of knowledge. It proceeded : such knowledge must be most necessary for us, and such knowledge is not attainable by the natural reason. This, says Duns, is confirmed by St Augustine, where he says in the third chapter of the eleventh book of the *De civitate Dei* that " we require outside evidence for the things which are beyond the scope of our senses and which we cannot know by any experience of our own."

And this passage, Duns continues, is a confirmation of the main argument of the preceding article. For since truths such as the Triunity of God, which were the subject of that article, are themselves intrinsically " neutral " to us, they are to be believed by no man on his own testimony concerning them ; a man must find the supernatural testimony of some being superior to the whole human species.

21d. But as to how such an original revelation or doctrine could have been made, or was made, says Duns, it is a matter of doubt whether it was by some inward voice or some audible speech, or by the proffering of some signs adequate to cause assent. It suffices, however, for the moment that such doctrine could be revealed in any of these ways. But in no case could the doctrine be passed on, in the first instance, by man without error.

Duns means presumably that whatever the mode of revelation, our knowledge remains imperfect by reason of the perversion of our natural faculties through the Fall.

22a. Duns now considers a possible objection which may be said to lie equally against all the three arguments which he has expounded, and which have been confirmed by St Augustine. These arguments, it may be said, are self-destructive. Take these matters which, as Duns has alleged, it is necessary for us to know. That which it is necessary for us to know must *eo ipso* be true, for nothing can be known unless it be true ; therefore whatever those arguments prove to the intellect to be necessary knowledge must be true. For instance, the proposition that the enjoyment of God is in itself man's end, which was put forward in the first argument [7], or the proposition that the way of attaining thereto is through merits which God accepts as worthy of such a reward, as put forth in the second argument [8], or the proposition that God is triune and that he acts contingently, as the third argument [13] alleges—all these propositions are shown to be true. Therefore we must say either that they have no basis except faith, or from them is to be drawn the opposite conclusion from that which they set out to prove.

22b. To this Duns replies by taking as illustration the proposition, " the enjoyment of God is man's end." The natural reason, he says, does not tell us that this proposition is necessarily true. It tells us that it is necessary for us to decide between the statement that the fruition of God is man's end and the statement that the fruition of God is not man's end. We must make up our minds on this issue ; yet it cannot be decided by the natural reason alone. So with respect to these other questions, the natural reason may present us with the dilemma, but cannot give the answer. Only faith can answer.

Article V

23. The fifth article disposes of the arguments of the philosophers. Their case [6] was that " man needs no supernatural knowledge in this life because he can derive all necessary knowledge for himself from the study of natural causes." They based themselves upon a number of passages in Aristotle. They argued first [6a] that the soul in knowing has two faculties, the active intellect and the passive or " possible " intellect. Knowledge arises when the active and " possible " intellects are brought together and nothing hinders their operation. These two elements are relative to all possible intelligibles, for anything that cannot be grasped by the active and " possible " intellects is *eo ipso* unintelligible. The operation of the active and " possible " intellects is a natural operation. All knowledge, therefore, is natural knowledge.

In reply Duns points out the insufficiency of saying that knowledge is solely a matter of the active and " possible " intellects. Knowledge, he says, depends upon two elements, the knowing soul and the object known, for, as St Augustine says in the ninth book of his work on the Trinity (ch. 18), " knowledge is born of the knower and the thing known." Let us grant, then, that on the side of the knower the active and " possible " intellects are adequate by nature to the knowledge of all intelligibles whatsoever. But on the side of the object known, as Aristotle says in the *De anima* (430^a, 1), the mind is like a bare tablet. So far as the mind is concerned, then, the agent in knowing is the active intellect. To this extent the philosophers are right, but they have left out of account the part played by the object in all knowing, in so far as the object must be active.

The philosophers had argued that a passive capacity in nature that has no active capacity corresponding to it would be meaningless, that the " possible " intellect is a passive capacity in nature with respect to all intelligibles whatsoever ; therefore there must be some natural active capacity corresponding with it ; from this it follows that our natural powers are sufficient for all intelligibles. To this Duns now replies in a passage of much obscurity. " Nature," he says, is used in two senses : sometimes, as in the second book of Aristotle's *Physics*, it is taken to be the intrinsic principle of motion or rest ; here " nature " would appear to mean the substance of all things that have their source of movement and rest in themselves. Sometimes, on the other hand, " nature " is taken to be an active natural principle ; by this Duns may be taken to mean the form which, for instance, is the cause of a plant's growth, and so that which the plant is to become. Here " nature " is distinguished from art. A work of art, he means, does not grow but is made by an extrinsic agent. Or " nature " in the sense of an active principle is distinguished from things caused in the opposite way, that is to say, not by growth, and this whether the cause be intrinsic to them or not, provided the cause be natural. Duns would seem to mean, for instance, that though a stone falls naturally, its falling is not natural in the sense of growth, and the cause of its falling is not intrinsic if, for example, I drop it. In whichever sense the word be taken, says Duns, the major premiss of the philosophers is false—namely, that every passive capacity in nature must have an active capacity in nature corresponding with it. It is false in the first sense, because " there are many things that are naturally receptive of some perfection whereof they do not possess the *intrinsic* active principle." We might say, perhaps, in illustration that a lump of clay is by nature receptive of the form of a goddess or a horse or whatever the moulder may make of it, but a lump of clay has no intrinsic natural principle corresponding to this form imposed upon it. The philosophers' major premiss is false also, says Duns, if nature be taken in the second sense, for there are cases where " a nature on account of its own excellence is naturally disposed for the reception of a perfection so eminent that it could not be subject to the causality of a natural agent as defined in the second sense ; and thus it is in the case before us." Duns means that the mind is naturally disposed to receive the vision of God, but this cannot be received by natural agency.

We are not to say, then, that a passive capacity in nature which had no active capacity corresponding to it would be meaningless, for, says Duns, " granted that in principle the passive capacity could not be brought to realisation by a natural agent, yet such a natural agent could induce a *disposition* to that realisation, and the passive capacity could be brought to realisation by some other agent in nature : that is, in the whole co-ordination of existences, as, for instance, through a supernatural agent." Duns's argument may, perhaps, be put thus : the passive or " possible " intellect is by nature capable of responding to all things that are intelligible. In the normal way of knowledge the passive intellect is " in-formed " by the active intellect—the active intellect impresses the " form " upon the " possible " intellect. But there are " forms " which are beyond the reach and attainment of the active intellect operating by its natural powers ; in these cases, however, the active intellect does not wholly cease to function ; its function is to induce in the passive intellect a " disposition " for the reception of the object beyond the scope of the natural reach of the active intellect. Thus, we cannot by thinking or studying nature come to know that God is triune, but we can by thinking be intellectually disposed to accept that truth when it is supernaturally made known to us—that is, through a supernatural agent.

But suppose the objection be made that according to Aristotle in the second book of the *De coelo et mundo* (290^a, 30) nature by no means falls short in nobler excellencies, whereas Duns's view " vilifies " nature as being unable of itself to achieve its own perfection from natural sources. To this Duns replies that " if our felicity really consisted in that highest speculative knowledge to which we can *now* attain *by natural means*, Aristotle would not say that nature is defective in things that are necessary. Now I grant that this highest speculative knowledge can be possessed naturally, but, beyond that, I say that there is another more eminent kind of knowledge that can be *naturally received.* Herein, therefore, nature receives a greater dignity than if the highest speculative knowledge were merely that which nature can give. Nor is there occasion for surprise if in some nature there be a passive capacity for a greater perfection than that to which its active causality extends, as is plain in the case of the human body." In other words, Duns's view exalts human nature ; it does not " vilify " it.

Besides, Duns continues, the reference to Aristotle's observation that nature does not fall short in nobler excellencies is nothing to the point ; for what he is discussing in that passage is physical organs that correspond to motor power. If there were such a power in the stars, he means, nature would have given them appropriate organs. " I grant it as a universal principle," says Duns, " that where we find a capacity that is designed to be organic, nature provides an appropriate organ—I mean, of course, in cases where there is no natural defect. But in the case before us we find a capacity but not such as to require an organ ; nature, however, does not provide all the other elements that beside the capacity concur to produce the realisation of the capacity. We may therefore take Aristotle to mean that what is naturally designed for some activity or object has by nature a capacity for that object, and the organ requisite for the activity if the power is an organic one, but that that is not the case so far as concerns the other requisites for action." Duns means that we may have by nature the organ for knowledge, but we may not have natural knowledge of a given object.

" There is something further to be said," Duns continues " about the philosophers' major premiss, namely, that there must be an active capacity at all points corresponding to a passive. That is quite true when we speak of the natural passive power as the passive is compared to the active ; but it is not true as the passive is compared to the activity received." This is related to the distinction made above [18] between the two meanings of the term " supernatural," which may either point to a supernatural operation of the intellect, which is not to be asserted, since all knowing is of the same kind, or to a supernatural agent such as an angel ; this is to be asserted.

In respect of the philosophers' minor premiss, namely that the " possible " intellect is a passive capacity in nature with respect to all things that are intelligible, Duns says that this is true in the second sense, not in the first ; that is to say, the natural reason can grasp any intellectual truth, but it cannot of itself, apart from supernatural help, attain all necessary truth. Or the philosophers' minor premiss might more readily be met by saying that, although in principle the possible intellect is naturally patient of such understanding, yet, as things are, it is not.

24a. Duns now turns to deal with the second argument of the philosophers [6b]. This was based upon Aristotle's assertion in the sixth book of the *Metaphysics* that all speculative knowledge falls under metaphysics, physics (or natural philosophy) and mathematics. Since these disciplines cover the whole field of speculative knowledge, it is argued that there is no need for supernatural revelation. Duns's reply is obscure to us because it is not to be translated into any familiar terms of modern thought. However, it begins simply enough. Things known by different kinds of reasoning, he says, lead to a diversity of sciences. For instance, the same conclusion may be proved, though in different ways, both by the astronomer and the physicist. Take the proposition that the earth is round ; whereas the astronomer proves his case by the medium of mathematics, that is, by abstraction from matter, the physicist's proof is by middle terms depending on observation and therefore concrete. Hence in respect of those things which the philosophical sciences treat according as the subject

48

matter is knowable by the light of the natural reason, nothing prevents another science from proving them also according as they are known by the light of divine revelation. No, but then it may be urged that, as regards things knowable in the field of theology, if there is a knowledge of them available or potentially available in other sciences, even though they are there seen in another light, there is no *necessity* for a knowledge of those things through theology. This may be illustrated by the example taken above : if a man knows from physics that the earth is round, he has no absolute need of a knowledge of the same fact by the abstract arguments of mathematics.

When Duns first put the case of the philosophers [6b], he said on their behalf that, in the light of Aristotle's assertion of the three modes of speculation that cover all possible knowledge, there seems to be no room for further modes of speculation. The word there translated or paraphrased as " modes " is *habitus*. It is literally to be translated a " having " or " habit " ; it is the Latin rendering of the word *hexis* used by Aristotle. *Habitus* has been defined, by Professor McKeon in his glossary, as " the quality which supervenes on potentiality and adheres permanently, aiding in the operation to which it is proper." Thus, when a man suddenly and for the first time falls in love, there is something or somebody that " informs " or awakens his passive potentiality to love. There then supervenes the habit or state or abiding disposition of being in love ; that is a " habit." Thus in different ways both various kinds of knowledge and various kinds of virtue are " habits." In the present context a " speculative habit " is really a quality of the trained mind.

Duns's technical and concentrated answer here to the philosophers' argument may be paraphrased thus : a " habit " is a quality (here a quality of mind) that is derived from the exercise of a faculty ; it is a quality that is a permanent possession of him who has it ; it helps him in the exercise of his faculty. If, for instance, a man is in the habit of reading philosophy, its terms and ideas are

familiar to him ; this " habit " therefore helps him whenever he takes up a philosophical book. But this " habit "
is also a " form," that is, it is a particular quality of mind,
specifically different from all other qualities of mind. In
so far as it is a quality of mind, it may be distinguished
from its object ; we distinguish, for instance, a philosophic
" habit " from philosophy. But in so far as this " habit "
is a " form "—that is, in its aspect as a quality of specific
difference from all other qualities—it may be distinguished
from an active principle ; that is, it is unrelated to the
exercise of a faculty. Now, with regard to a scientific
quality or " habit " of mind, principles are the efficient
causes of its being a scientific habit of mind. Granted,
then, that where the same fact is knowable through two
disciplines—as, for instance, that of the mathematician
and that of the physicist in respect of the roundness of
the earth—there is no distinction in respect of the object,
the round earth, yet there is a distinction in respect
of the principles whereby mathematician and physicist
respectively reach their common conclusion. There
is, then, a distinction of " habits " in so far as they are
" forms," but not in so far as they are " habits."

To this it may be replied that " form " as more
inclusive is a higher category than " habit," since every
" habit " is a " form," but not every " form " is a " habit."
" Form," that is, stands in relation to " habit " as the
universal to the particular. Now, it is impossible that
things should be distinct in regard to a more comprehensive category and indistinguishable in respect of a less
comprehensive category ; it is impossible, for instance,
that two creatures should be distinguishable as animals
but not as men. It is likewise impossible that they should
be distinguished as " forms " but indistinguishable as
" habits." Further, if causes of distinction have any
relation to those " habits," only efficient causes can be
in question, and these are principles ; but the argument
we are refuting assumes that the causes of distinction are
objects and that these act as formal or final causes. Besides,

" however much one can assume different ' habits ' of knowledge, one cannot prove the necessity of one particular ' habit,' as if knowledge were impossible apart from it— assuming, that is, the possibility of another ' habit ' from some source or other." If it be conceded that different " habits " are possible, we cannot prove that a super- natural " habit " of knowledge is necessary—it being assumed that we can have knowledge of the same object from some other source.

24b. Duns now briefly gives his own answer. It is that, even if those speculative sciences deal with all matters about which speculative thought is possible, yet they do not deal with these matters in respect of everything that is knowable about them, because they do not deal with them in respect of their knowable *special* properties. Here he refers back to what he had said above [13], that speculative knowledge is concerned with universals, not with particulars. Granted, we may say, that metaphysics treats of the divine, we cannot by studying metaphysics know God as we need to know him.

25. Duns comes now to the third argument of the philosophers, namely, that the knowledge of conclusions depends simply upon the understanding of the principle and the deduction of the conclusion therefrom ; if, there- fore, principles are understood, and the deduction from them is plain to see, nothing further is required for the knowledge of the conclusion ; further, we do know by the light of nature the first principles wherein all knowable conclusions are virtually included ; therefore by the light of nature we can know all those knowable conclusions.

25a. Before he comes to his own reply Duns considers and rejects various suggested answers. First of all, then, some people might reply that " to some conclusions first principles cannot be applied unless those conclusions are in the field of things of sense, partly because the terms of those principles are drawn from things of sense, and therefore they smack of the nature of sensible things, and partly because the active intellect, through which must

be made the application of the conclusions to the principles, is limited to the things of sense." This, says Duns,
is unsatisfactory, since " it is a matter of certainty to the
intellect that those first principles are valid not only in
respect of the things of sense but also in respect of things
that are not of sensible perception ; for we no more doubt
in the case of immaterial things than in the case of material
things that contradictories cannot be true at the same
time concerning the same thing.   Hence the reply is
null."

25b. Much the same point, says Duns, may be put by
others in a somewhat different form, namely, that " the
term of a first principle is ' being,' which is divided into
ten categories, and that does not extend to the object
of theology."   That is to say, every first principle is about
a something, and every something must fall under one of
Aristotle's categories ; it must be a substance or a quality
or a relation or some such thing.   But Aristotle's ten
categories do not cover the Being of God ; therefore we
cannot deduce truths about God from first principles
which we already know.   " This argument has no validity,"
says Duns, " for we no more doubt in the case of God
than in any other case that contradictories are not simultaneously true.   We no more doubt, for instance, that
' God is blessed ' and ' God is not blessed ' or ' God is
true ' and ' God is not true ' are propositions which
cannot be true at the same time than we doubt in the case
of black and white."

25c. Another possible reply to be considered is this :
" conclusions do not follow simply from major premisses
but from major premisses to which minor premisses have
been added.   Now the minor premisses to be added are
not manifest by the light of natural reason, and they
must first be joined to the major before we can reach
a conclusion."   A modern instance will illustrate this
point (for Duns gives none) : war between brothers is
a very great evil : war between India and Pakistan would
be a war between brothers : therefore war between India

and Pakistan would be a very great evil. Here we know
the first principle that war between brothers is a great
evil, but we could not draw the conclusion that war
between India and Pakistan is a great evil till someone
had told us that war between India and Pakistan would
be a war between brothers. The conclusion, thus, is
something which cannot be deduced from the first principle itself. We must, therefore, reject the argument of
the philosophers that he who understands the terms of the
first principle can by the light of reason deduce all the
conclusions that follow from it. Duns rejects this argument also. He says, " the minor premisses that are to
be taken under the first principles predicate concerning
things taken under the terms that are subjects of the first
principles ; but it is known that the terms of the first
principles apply to all particulars because they are universally expressed " ; we may not, therefore, argue in
this way that conclusions cannot be deduced by those
who understand the terms of first principles. If, that is
to say, we really do know that all wars between brothers
are a great evil, then we do know that war between India
and Pakistan would be a great evil, for the minor premiss
is simply an illustration of the major and is contained in
it ; we could not strictly know the major if we did not
already know the minor.

We may comment here that this argument is related
to one of the criticisms of syllogistic reasoning often raised
in recent years. If we take quantitatively the major
premiss of our syllogism, " all war between brothers is
a great evil," then indeed the minor premiss is implied
in the major, and we should not be able to assert the
major if we did not antecedently know the minor. But,
as it has been argued, we might take the major premiss
in another way, not as a summary of instances, but as the
assertion of a perceived connexion between subject and
predicate. If the major premiss means, " we perceive
an essential connexion between the subject, 'war between
brothers,' and the predicate, ' a great evil,' " then the

minor premiss does in fact add something not asserted in the major. But Duns here, it appears, did not accept this solution.

25d. We come, therefore, to his own answer which is obscure to us in its medieval terminology. " As the terms of the subject are common (or universal)," he writes, " so also are the terms of the predicate ; when, therefore, the terms of the predicate being thus distributed are accepted in respect of all instances, they are accepted only in regard to the terms that are predicated ; these are most common (or universal) ; in consequence only the most common (or universal) predicates are known of the things that fall under these common terms in virtue of such principles." Duns's meaning may perhaps become clearer from an illustration. If the proposition " all men are mortal " is true, mortality may be predicated of every instance of man ; but we cannot go further and infer that all men are fair-haired or dark-haired, because in these subsidiary or inferior particulars of their manhood men greatly differ. That is to say, in logical argument subject and predicate must have the same generality, and general concepts are always abstract from particular individual characteristics. Thus from the first principle " all men are animals " we cannot infer that man is a laughing animal. But we can infer " man is a laughing animal " when a new middle term has been introduced and our first principle runs, " man is a rational animal " ; but from the proposition " man is a rational and therefore a laughing animal " we cannot infer that other animals laugh, for the capacity to laugh is contained virtually in rationality, but not in animality. There are, then, many truths about man that may be known though these cannot be derived from the first principle, " man is an animal." Duns offers an illustration : if we know that " the whole is greater than the part," we can deduce from this that four parts are greater than two parts in respect of the same object of predication. But the principle, " the whole is greater than the parts," does not include the proposition,

" four parts are twice two," or " three are one and a half times two." In order to prove these latter propositions we should need some special middle terms. If, then, the whole is greater than the parts, we know that three parts are greater than two, but we do not know all that is knowable about the relation of three parts to two ; our knowledge, so to put it, is general, not particular. Duns then puts the case in logical terms ; one can, he says, " descend " from the subject of a sentence that is an universal affirmative, but one cannot so " descend " from the predicate. Thus from the proposition " all men are animals," to revert to our illustration, we may " descend " from the subject and infer that John Doe and Richard Roe are animals, but we cannot " descend " from the predicate and infer that all men are " tigers " or " lions."

To this Duns thinks it may be replied that " in every proposition either affirmation or negation is necessarily true ; in no case can affirmation and negation be simultaneously true. From the necessity, therefore, that ' this is white or not white ' it follows that one may ' descend ' from the predicate as well as from the subject." To this he answers that we may know in general that a particular thing is either white or not white, but this knowledge does not enable us to determine which of the two it is ; that can only be determined by one who has seen it or learns from someone who has seen it. Duns offers a further illustration. The law of contradiction enables us to assert that man either is or is not a laughing creature, but whether in fact he is or is not a laughing creature requires a further premiss, such, for instance, as that risibility is a consequence of rationality.

26. In the concluding section of this question Duns reverts to the three main arguments set forth in the beginning [3] to show that man needs no supernatural doctrine.

26a. The first argument was : every faculty which has for its primary natural object some common field is adequate to all that is contained in that field as being its natural object : the intellect is a faculty that has for its primary natural object a common field : therefore the intellect is adequate to all that is contained in that field, namely the realm of the intelligible, as being its natural object ; it would follow, therefore, that no supernatural knowledge is necessary to man.

Before propounding his own solution Duns sets forth an answer which others might give, They might point out that the phrase " its natural object " is patient of two meanings. It might be taken of that to which the faculty can attain naturally or as the result of the action of causes that operate in the field of nature. Alternatively, it might be taken of that to which the faculty is by nature inclined, whether or not it can naturally attain thereto. The argument, then, is this : the major premiss is that every faculty which has for its primary natural object some common field is adequate to all that is contained in that field ; this premiss might be denied if it be taken in the first sense, namely, that the faculty can by its natural powers or by causes normally operative compass the whole field of its primary natural object ; for, the argument runs, the primary object exactly corresponds with the faculty, and is, therefore, abstracted from all those things about which the faculty can operate ; but such knowledge is general, and, granted that the intellect can by its natural powers have such general understanding, it does not follow that the intellect can by its natural powers understand everything that lies within that field ; for the understanding of some particular element in the field is a form of understanding far superior to the con-fused understanding of the field in general. The minor premiss was that " the intellect is a faculty which has for its primary natural object a common field," but in which-ever sense we take the phrase " its primary natural object," the conclusion does not follow—in the sense, that is, of the natural object being attainable by the natural powers of the intellect, for in this regard the major premiss was false.

Duns repudiates this argument as self-destructive ; for

the primary object of a faculty exactly corresponds with that faculty. This is not to be gainsaid : a faculty looks to nothing as its object unless it falls under that primary object, and wherever the nature of that primary object is found, there the faculty regards it as its object. The argument, therefore, that the intellect might grasp the general field in a diffuse way but be inadequate to particulars in that field is impossible ; no field can be a primary object naturally without everything contained in that field being intrinsically a natural object of that faculty. For, if that be denied, the primary object does not exactly correspond with the faculty universally or naturally ; it goes beyond the faculty and something less than it exactly corresponds with the faculty ; it is this something less that will be the primary object of the faculty.

The fallacy called " figure of speech " consists in a confusion between the ordinary and a metaphorical use of a word or phrase. This fallacy, says Duns, is illustrated by the foregoing argument where a " this " and a " like this " are confused. Thus, " granted that the intellect can naturally attain to the understanding of a thing as something intelligible by a single act, as, for instance, ' man ' is intelligible by a single act of the intellect (for this single act of intellection grasping a thing as a single object is natural) ; yet it does not follow that the primary object, which exactly corresponds with the faculty, namely ' being,' can be posited as a primary object naturally attainable by the intellect unless every object contained under it is so attainable ; for it is the primary object precisely as it is involved in all the objects that fall under it. When, therefore, it is argued that a ' being ' is naturally attainable by the intellect, and therefore ' being ' as the primary object exactly corresponding with the faculty is naturally attainable by the intellect, a ' this ' has been changed into ' a thing of this kind ' ; for the antecedent is true in the sense of one single intelligible thing, such as ' white,' while the consequent draws the conclusion

57

concerning ' being ' as it is involved in every intelligible, not as it is understood apart from these."

26b. We come, therefore, in the end to Duns's own personal solution of the question. The real reply to the argument, he says, is different. The minor premiss in the syllogism was, " the intellect is a faculty which has for its primary natural object a common field." This minor premiss is false in respect of the natural object understood as naturally attainable ; but it is true in another sense, that is, if we take the natural object to be that towards which the capacity is naturally disposed.

Duns finds confirmation of his view in what St Anselm writes in the second chapter of his book *De libero arbitrio*. " As I suppose," wrote Anselm, " we have no power which by itself would suffice for its own realisation." What he calls " power " continues Duns, is what we usually call " capacity," as becomes plain from his illustration taken from the sense of sight. It is not unsuitable, therefore, that a capacity should be naturally intended for an object to which it cannot naturally attain as a result of natural causes, just as every capacity is directed of itself alone to its realisation, and yet cannot attain thereto of itself alone.

27. With the second principal argument Duns deals very briefly. The argument [3b] was that if even in the case of inferior faculties, that is the senses, nature supplies whatever they need to fulfil their purposes and achieve their ends, *a fortiori* nature supplies a superior faculty, the intellect, with all that it needs to fulfil its function and attain its end. This argument was based on Aristotle's assertion in the *De anima* that " nature does not fail in things that are necessary." With this citation Duns has already dealt [23], where he pointed out that Aristotle would be justified in his view, if, or in so far as, our felicity depends upon the highest speculative knowledge to which we can now naturally attain. He now repeats that " superior things are intended for the passive reception of a greater perfection than they can actively produce ;

hence their perfection cannot be produced except by some supernatural agent. It is otherwise with the perfection of inferior things, for their final perfection can follow from the action of inferior agents."

28. Finally Duns comes to the third principal argument [3c]. The argument was this : " if any supernaturally revealed doctrine be necessary, this must be because strictly within the limits of nature the faculty of the intellect is disproportionate to the object as thus knowable. It follows, therefore, that the faculty must be made proportionate to its object by means of something other than itself. This something other is either something natural or something supernatural. If it is something natural, the natural intellect with the natural addition will still be disproportionate to the primary object. If this additional something is supernatural, the natural faculty for that reason is disproportionate to it. Hence, once again, it can only become proportionate to it by means of something else—and so *ad infinitum*. Since, then, as Aristotle shows in the second book of the *Metaphysics*, an infinite regress is impossible, we must abide by the original position that the faculty of the intellect is itself proportionate to everything that is knowable and is itself capable of every kind of knowledge in respect of every mode of its knowability."

In regard to this third argument, says Duns, " I say that the ' possible ' intellect is disproportionate to the firm grasp of some complex truth," (such, we may interpolate, as God's Triunity) ; " that is to say, in respect of such agents as cannot be known from images and from the natural light of the active intellect, the ' possible ' intellect is not a thing that can be made proportionate to that which moves it. But when you argue, ' then it is made proportionate by something else,' I agree with you. But it is made proportionate through the instrumentality of something else of the nature of a mover, for the ' possible ' intellect gives assent to that truth through some supernatural mover that reveals it. Also the ' possible ' intellect is made proportionate through something else in the nature of a ' form,' for it takes place through the assent wrought in the ' possible ' intellect, which is a kind of inclination in the intellect to that object, an inclination which makes the ' possible ' intellect proportionate to it. When, further, you ask that other question, whether the agent be natural or supernatural, I reply ' supernatural,' and that whether you are thinking of the agent or the ' form.' When, therefore, you draw the inference that the intellect is disproportionate thereto and is made proportionate through the instrumentality of something else, my reply is that the ' possible ' intellect in itself has a capacity for obedience to the agent, and thus is sufficiently proportionate to the agent so far as concerns its being moved thereby. Similarly the intellect is of itself capable of that assent which is caused by such an agent and is *naturally capable* of it. In receiving such a truth, therefore, the intellect does not need to be made proportionate to that assent by anything else."

The argument might be thus set out in modern terms : the eye by its own natural powers observes what is happening in its neighbourhood ; it cannot by its natural powers see that which happened long ago or is happening at a distance. But under special influences, which we may call supernatural or psychic, the eye is given a " second sight " and sees that which by its natural powers it cannot see. Here that which is given, the " form," is not that which is naturally available to the eye, and the agent that impresses this " form " upon the eye is not the normal agent in seeing. But while the eye is not naturally capable of seeing these things remote in time or space, it is naturally capable of being made to see them under certain circumstances. So it is with the intellect, as Duns maintains. In all ordinary knowing the mind is stimulated by the world of sense, and the " forms " which it receives are those derived from the world of sense. Thus, for instance, the mind can naturally attain to the knowledge of the law of gravitation ; but it cannot naturally attain to the truth that God sent his Son into the world. Only the Spirit of God can bring this truth before the sight of the mind ; the truth itself, the " form," is supernatural in that it is not derived from the world of sense, and the agent is supernatural, namely, the Spirit of God. But we avoid the infinite regress, to which the philosophers' argument pointed, by the assertion that, though the mind could not of itself attain that truth, it is naturally capable of receiving it when the appropriate supernatural agent imposes it upon the mind. The mind, then, can immediately apprehend the spiritual or supernatural truth ; no mediation is required.

The phrase " its natural object," as has been pointed out, might be taken in either of two senses ; it might mean " that to which the faculty can attain naturally or by the action of causes that are naturally active," or, alternatively, it might mean " that towards which the faculty is naturally inclined, whether or not it could naturally attain the object." The supernatural truth that we need to know, says Duns, is the natural object of the intellect in the second sense, but not in the first. In the first sense the revealed truth has not sufficient force to incline the intellect to give its assent ; thus both on the side of the agent and of the mind that is to receive we have a disproportion. But, while the revealed truth has not sufficient force to incline the intellect to give its assent, the supernatural agent has sufficient force to incline the intellect to that truth by causing in it an assent whereby it is made proportionate to this truth in such a way that the intellect requires no other medium whereby it may be made proportionate to such an agent nor to the " form " thereby impressed.

Epilogue

In this sudden and unemotional way the long argument
ends. It has been an exercise in logic, and is in structure
wholly academic. It may be well by way of epilogue to
indicate wherein, as may be thought, the question presents
itself to us today in quite other terms, and from that point
of view briefly to comment upon some of the issues raised
by Duns.

Duns's question has been, " is it necessary for man in
this present life that he receive by inspiration some special
doctrine, unavailable to him by the light of the natural
reason ? " The word translated " doctrine " is *doctrina*.
Duns does not ask whether man in this present life needs
the light of revelation ; he asks whether man needs supernatural " doctrine." It is assumed by him, and by many
still, that revelation takes the form of doctrine. We might
agree with Duns that man needs light from beyond this
passing world and exceeding the knowledge offered in the
natural sciences if he is to guide his feet aright through
life, while we might sorrowfully admit that supernatural
information is not given him. Revelation does not, and
cannot, take the form of doctrine, though it may be
adumbrated, and, in some sense, preserved in doctrine.

Every faculty, the philosophers argue [3a], which
has for its primary natural object some common field, is
adequate to all that is contained in that field as its intrinsic
natural object. But, we may ask, is the eye, even when
fortified by every instrument that science has invented or
shall invent, adequate to the whole field of the visible ?
Is the eye of itself sufficient to see all that may be seen ?
I may see the distant scene as clearly as it may be
represented by a camera with a first-rate lens, but, if I see
it as the camera may be said to see it, I do not see it as
the artist sees it, and when later I see his painting of it,
I am as one whose eyes have been opened so that I see

63

with new eyes or see that which I never saw before. Another light than that of the sun, we might say, is needful that we may see all that may be seen. Similarly we might say that the intellect is adequate to all intelligibles, and yet how much more than mere intellect is needed that intelligible things be understood ! " The rest may reason and wonder ; 'tis we musicians know." It may be that mathematics and all sciences in so far as they are abstract and dependent upon mathematics may be grasped by the intellect alone ; but in all human affairs, and in all judgements of value, and wherever wisdom is required beyond bare cleverness, the powers of the brain, so to put it, unless they be strengthened and fortified by the powers of the heart, are not adequate to all intelligibles. The eye is adequate to all the field of the visible, the intellect to the whole field of the intelligible ; yet neither of itself can the eye see all that is to be seen, nor of itself can the intellect grasp all that must be understood. In both cases it is not improper to speak of " revelation," but " revelation " takes the form of insight, not of " doctrine." We may agree with Duns, then, as against St Thomas, that there is only one kind of knowing, and that the natural intellect is of itself sufficient for all intelligibles, and we may agree with Duns that all knowledge comes through the things of sense ; but rather than claim that supernatural information is imparted to us, we might prefer to say that beauty and meaning are a kind of interpenetration of the natural by the supernatural. " The Word became flesh," we read, " and tabernacled amongst us, and we beheld his glory." But not all beheld his glory. Some said, " is not this the carpenter ? " and others, " he hath a devil." The doctrine of the divinity of Christ is not a matter of revelation ; it is a comment on the revelation.

The same principle may be illustrated from the sphere of ethics. If I see a child fall into the river, I know that I should jump in to pull it out. The sense of obligation is not apart from the seeing, but is not derived from the seeing. Through, and not apart from, the sensible I am aware of the supersensible. In Duns's terms, the active intellect cannot inform the " possible " intellect of that which does not come from the sensible. The sense of obligation is super-natural, if the natural is the sensible ; but the supernatural knowledge does not come in the form of a proposition ; the revelation, so to call it, is in the imperative, not the indicative, mood : " jump in." Duns, we may suppose, would not agree with this ; he would maintain that this principle of obligation is a first principle apprehended by the natural reason. That we need not question, but this is only because the unsophisticated natural reason is open to a world that is supernatural in the sense of supersensible. When, therefore, the philosopher is supposed to say [6a] that " the ' possible ' intellect is designed by nature to seek the knowledge of everything knowable, this is achieved in a natural way by whatever cognition it may be ; the ' possible ' intellect is, therefore, adapted by its nature to every kind of act of the understanding," we may agree, but we should wish to add that the " possible " intellect, to keep to this term, is open to the super-sensible or supernatural as well as to the natural or sensible at all times and in all things.

Thus we do not agree with the philosopher whom Duns has in mind or with the modern scientist whom we have in mind. The philosopher is deemed to say [6] that " man in this present life has no need of supernatural knowledge, since he can acquire all the knowledge necessary to him by a consideration of the working of natural causes." This is the very philosophy of modern secularism, which maintains that there is no knowledge except scientific knowledge, and scientific knowledge is derived wholly through a study of natural causes ; all other alleged types of knowledge are subjective, unreliable, relative, a matter of taste, and not really knowledge. That is to say, when the child falls into the water, I do not know, I only think I know, that I should jump in after it ; when I assert that Milton is superior to Ella Wheeler Wilcox as a poet, I am not expressing a fact but only a private judgement. But in truth the modern secularist has, and must have for the purposes of life, much knowledge which is not solely an inference from sensible facts but which, though derived from sensible experience, is supersensible and relative to insight. We need revelation in the sense of super-natural or super-sensible knowledge, but it is not vouchsafed to us, as Duns supposed, in the form of heavenly information. The natural and the super-natural, the sensible and the super-sensible, are given us together in experience. Revelation, in its religious aspect, does not come to us in the form of propositions or of dogmas or doctrines, but in the awareness of God through nature and through history.

Much of this is relevant to the philosopher's contention [3b] that since no supernatural aid is needed by the senses for the apprehension of their objects, therefore the intellect needs none. One further comment may be allowed. It seems to be presupposed that the senses and the intellect are comparable to a beam of light from a lantern which, turning in every direction, can bring to knowledge all that there is to be revealed. This corresponds to our inveterate tendency to write as though things and propositions are the only objects of knowledge. Things and propositions are not affected by being known, and, apart from insight, sharpness of senses or of intellect would appear the only requisites for knowledge. But knowledge of persons is a very different matter. Friendship is a type of knowledge which does not conform to these standards. No man can be known in friendship unless, as we say, he " gives himself away " to his friend. Certain qualities, too, are required in the knower, as there must be some initiative on the part of the known. So, when we come to the spheres of the ethical, the spiritual and the aesthetic as well as the personal, we find the insufficiency of mere physical sensitivity and intellectual acumen. This may be an indication that in all these spheres we are aware of a personal universe ; a personal universe spells revelation, but not supernaturally imparted information.

I have already commented briefly on the third argument which Duns [3c] puts into the mouth of the philosopher, that if supernaturally revealed doctrine were necessary, this must be because strictly within the limits of nature the faculty of the intellect is disproportionate to the object as thus knowable ; the faculty, therefore, must be made proportionate by means of something other than itself, and here we come to an infinite regress. I suggested that the argument is cogent against those who maintain that the finite has no capacity whatever to receive the infinite, and that God is the Wholly Other. But, further, the presupposition of this as of so much of the argument is that we either know divine truth or we do not know it, divine truth being in the form of propositions which must be accepted or rejected. But it is wiser to speak in terms of insight. No man is *totally* impervious to the supernatural or supersensible environment that surrounds us, at least not by nature, and there is room for immeasurably varied degrees of insight. For instance, it is part of the common tradition of Aryan-speaking peoples that God is Father ; they spoke of *Dyaus pitar*, of *Zeus pater*, of *Jupiter*. If we may be said to apprehend the Fatherhood of God, it can only be because God has so revealed himself. There is, no doubt, a very great difference between those who accept and those who reject this belief, but how great may be the difference between those who suppose that they accept it ! To one it appears almost as a truism, to another as a probable hypothesis, to a third as a statement about a benevolent Providence, to a fourth as a wonder beyond wonder ; one man sees as deeply into a mystery as man can, another sees so superficially and dimly that he scarcely seems to see at all. Revelation is not a matter of the acceptance or rejection of logical propositions but a matter of insight patient of almost infinite degrees.

Duns's long argument is throughout dominated by the conception of logic as deductive reasoning. The philosopher, therefore, can argue that all possible conclusions are logically implied in first principles which are in most general terms [6c]. The scientific method, as we understand it, proceeds in the opposite way. It does not start from general first principles from which it deduces concerning particulars ; rather, it starts from particulars and moves forward from them to general propositions. Each mode of arguing, the deductive and the inductive, has its place in logical thinking, but the change that in this matter has come over science has a parallel in a change that has come over theology for modern men. It would no doubt be monstrously convenient for the theologian to receive from heaven a number of supernaturally revealed propositions to form the major premisses of his syllogisms, and there are, indeed, many theologians who still suppose themselves to enjoy these great advantages. But the Bible is not a handbook of theology in that sense. Primarily it tells a story of the merciful ways of God with man ; it is concerned with events rather than with theorems and with particulars which cannot provide the kind of major premiss once presupposed. But if neither scientists nor theologians receive information direct from heaven, it is well that they should not forget that they can only start their thinking from first principles, which themselves are neither scientific nor theological truths but insights of the natural reason.

When Duns [7] turns to reply to his philosopher, he lays it down as a first principle that " every rational agent requires a clear apprehension of its proper end." And, indeed, it might seem obvious that unless we know precisely where we want to go, we are not likely to reach our appointed destination. Duns argues that if a man cannot derive from nature, as in fact he cannot, a distinct knowledge of his end, such knowledge must be supernaturally imparted to him. But we may properly raise the question whether the Christian faith actually offers

us a distinct knowledge of our end. " Brethren, now are
we children of God, and it doth not yet appear what we
shall be." That we are totally without knowledge of our
end, that Scripture leaves us totally in the dark, that the
mind of seers and of saints is here totally unilluminated,
is not to be maintained. But clear and distinct knowledge
is another matter. We must walk by faith, not by sight
nor by that kind of knowledge which is not of faith. John
Oman has written of our duty to go forward through life
" with a compass in one hand and a sword in the other "
—with a compass, not with a map.

In the New Testament " faith " nearly always means
fides qua creditur, not *fides quae creditur*, the act of the person
whereby he believes, not the substance or content of
belief ; it is an act of self-committal ; it is trust in a
Person, a personal relationship. For Duns, as for many
still, faith is pre-eminently the intellectual acceptance of
orthodox doctrine taken to be supernaturally guaranteed,
the acceptance of propositions, not an attitude to the
Person who has evoked our trust. It may often be found
that an insistence upon the necessity for information supernaturally guaranteed marches with a deep inner scepticism,
that is, with the conviction that without revelation of that
kind we know nothing. But we need not walk in dark-
ness, even if much is still hidden from us. Duns argues
[7b] that we can only infer the proper end of any
substance from a consideration of its manifest activities ;
in man's case we cannot infer his supernatural end from
his manifest activities ; or, even if it be the case that the
natural reason points to the vision of God as man's
natural end, yet at least the natural reason gives us no
assurance of particulars such as a bodily resurrection or
a permanence of the vision such as is required by us if
we ordinary mortals are fervently to desire and to pursue
this true end of our nature. We are disposed to reply
that Duns demands precisely that kind of assurance which
we are not given. Assurance may be ours indeed, but
it springs from perfect trust in a Person whom in measure

at least we know, not from guaranteed information, a supernatural map supernaturally provided. Revelation is the correlative of trust, not of an act of intellectual surrender to propositions set forth as authoritative. Here we know in part ; we see through a glass darkly, but we see.

Duns [8] argues further that " beatitude is vouch-safed as if it were a reward for merit to him whom God accepts as if the recipient were worthy of such a reward " ; hence blessedness is not the inevitable result of any of our activities ; it is given by God " contingently," that is, according to Duns, by the arbitrary will of God ; there-fore it cannot be known by the light of the natural reason ; therefore we need supernatural knowledge. Here Duns hovers round an issue of first importance for our question. He was concerned with the " contingent " will of God rather than with " the sure mercies of David " ; but we may revise his doctrine in the form that the Gospel is not to be discovered by any process of thinking ; moreover, no study of human nature or of the activities of man will yield the Gospel. The Gospel, therefore, is of revelation ; but it is of revelation in the Person and work, the life, the death, the resurrection of Jesus Christ, not in the form of propositions ; he is the revelation ; he is the ground of assurance ; faith is trust in him. When Duns argues that by the light of nature we cannot know *all* the things necessary to our final end, we may well think of Luther who made so plain that we know the one thing necessary to our final end, namely, faith in Christ alone.

Duns argues [13] from Aristotle's *Metaphysics* that we cannot have a metaphysic of the qualities proper to spiritual substances. His thought might, perhaps, be represented in such modern terms as these : science deals with the sensible world ; God or the angels cannot be the subject of scientific inquiry, and only to a limited extent can they be the subject of metaphysical inquiry, for metaphysical knowledge is in terms of universals ; metaphysics does not deal with particulars or individual entities. This is an issue treated particularly in De Burgh's posthumous treatise, *The Life of Reason*. It is part of our inheritance from Aristotle, he there points out, that we tend to regard the individual as unknowable ; we can describe it in universal terms but its individuality eludes us. We can, that is, only describe an object in terms that are applicable to other things as well, such as " white," " round," " sweet," " translucent," and the like ; we can only define in terms of genus and of species ; scientific knowledge is in general terms of law, and is only concerned with the individual as illustrating law. Metaphysics we take to be yet more abstract ; it treats of truth, goodness and beauty, but these are abstractions from the concretes where these qualities are exemplified. But God is not the great Abstraction ; he is the living God ; he is concrete ; he is he. Metaphysics, therefore, may tell us something *about* God, but cannot apprehend God. So Duns may be supposed to argue, and the argument would seem valid against his philosopher, even though its assumptions are now criticised by some. But it may be thought that Duns's argument would take him further than he saw. If revelation is the revelation of God, not an Abstraction but a Person, it can hardly take the form of *doctrine*, though, no doubt, doctrine is involved when men try to express that which they have seen.

Duns did not suppose that doctrine could be declared in human speech without any admixture of error [31], but he clearly supposed that dogma itself is revealed. Thus he assumes the traditional doctrine of the Trinity, and explains that this doctrine could never have been derived from the data of sensible perception ; indeed, the study of things sensible positively misleads us in respect of the Trinity, for it affords no parallel and suggests another doctrine [13] ; therefore the orthodox doctrine must be supernaturally revealed. Naturally he does not contemplate our modern questions, but he drops a serviceable hint [21] which he does not develop. Speaking of the original revelation he says it is a matter of doubt whether it was made by some inward voice or some audible speech or by the proffering of some " signs " adequate to cause assent. What had he in mind when he spoke of these " signs " ? We might desire to say that God has not delivered to us doctrine in so many words but has provided us with " signs," for those who have eyes to see ; pre-eminent, of course, among these " signs " is the coming and the person of Christ, and it is from these " signs " that man has constructed the doctrines which are now called orthodox.

Latin Text

B. Ioannis Duns Scoti super prologum magistri sententiarum quaestio prima [1]

PROLOGUS

1. Circa prologum huius primi libri Sententiarum quaeruntur quinque. Primum de necessitate huius doctrinae, et spectat ad genus causae efficientis ; et est quaestio : utrum necessarium sit homini pro statu isto aliquam doctrinam specialem supernaturaliter inspirari ? Secundum spectat ad genus causae formalis, et est quaestio: utrum cognitio supernaturalis necessaria viatori tradita sit sufficienter in sacra scriptura ? Tertium spectat ad genus causae materialis, et est quaestio : utrum theologia sit de Deo tanquam de subiecto primo ? Quartum et quintum pertinent ad genus causae finalis, et est quarta quaestio : utrum theologia sit practica ? Quinta vero quaestio : utrum ex ordine ad praxim ut ad finem dicatur per se scientia practica ?

QUAESTIO I

2. Primo quaeritur : *utrum homini pro statu isto sit necessarium aliquam doctrinam specialem supernaturaliter inspirari, ad quam videlicet non possit attingere lumine naturali intellectus ?*

3. Et videtur quod non, sic : (**a**) omnis potentia habens aliquod commune pro primo obiecto naturali potest in quodlibet contentum sub illo sicut in per se obiectum naturale. Hoc patet per exemplum de primo obiecto visus et aliis contentis sub illo, et ita inductive in aliis obiectis

---

[1] The text printed here is that which I have translated and paraphrased. It is not based upon a meticulous collation of all available manuscripts and editions but is offered as a sufficient working text ; it is based upon the critical Quaracchi edition and differs from it in no important particular.

N. M.

primis et potentiis. Patet etiam per rationem, quia
primum obiectum dicitur quod est adaequatum potentiae ;
sed si in aliquo esset ratio eius, scilicet primi obiecti, circa
quod non posset potentia habere actum naturaliter,
obiectum non esset potentiae adaequatum sed obiectum
excederet potentiam. Patet ergo maior. Sed primum
obiectum intellectus nostri naturale est ens in quantum
ens ; ergo intellectus noster potest naturaliter habere
actum circa quodcumque ens, et sic circa quodcumque
intelligibile, etiam circa non ens, quia negatio cognoscitur
per affirmationem ; *ergo*, etc. Probatio minoris : Avic.
I Metaphys., C. v. ens et res prima impressione imprimuntur
in animam, nec possunt manifestari ex aliis : si autem
esset aliquid aliud ab istis primum obiectum, ista possent
manifestari per rationem illius, sed hoc est impossibile,
ergo. . . .

(**b**) Praeterea, sensus non indiget aliqua cognitione
supernaturali pro isto statu, ergo nec intellectus. Antecedens patet. Probatio consequentiae : natura non
deficit in necessariis, III *de anima*. Et si in imperfectis non
deficit, multo magis nec in perfectis. Ergo si non deficit
in potentiis inferioribus quantum ad necessaria eis, propter
actus suos habendos et finem earum consequendum, multo
magis non deficit in necessariis potentiae superiori ad
actum suum et finem consequendum ; *ergo*, etc.

(**c**) Praeterea, si aliqua talis doctrina sit necessaria,
hoc est quia potentia in puris naturalibus est improper-
tionata obiecto ut sic cognoscibili ; ergo oportet quod per
aliquid aliud a se fiat ei proportionata. Illud aliud aut
est naturale aut supernaturale. Si est naturale, ergo totum
est improportionatum obiecto primo. Si supernaturale,
ergo potentia est improportionata illi ; et ita sequitur
quod per aliud oportet ei proportionari, et sic in infinitum.
Cum ergo non sit procedere in infinitum, II *Metaphys.*,

oportet stare in primo, dicendo quod potentia intellectiva sit ex se proportionata omni cognoscibili et secundum omnem modum cognoscibilis ; *quare*, etc.

4. II Tim. III, xvi : omnis scriptura divinitus inspirata utilis est ad docendum, ad arguendum, ad corripiendum in iustitia, ut perfectus sit homo Dei, etc. Praeterea, Baruch III, xxxi sqq., de sapientia dicitur : non est qui possit scire vias eius ; sed qui scit universa novit eam. Ergo nullus alius potest habere eam nisi a sciente universa. Hoc quantum ad necessitatem eius. De facto subdit : Tradidit eam Iacob puero suo et Israel dilecto suo. Hoc quantum ad vetus Testamentum. Et sequitur : Post haec in terris visus est, et cum hominibus conversatus est, scilicet quando tradidit eam, quoad novum Testamentum.

ARTICULUS I

5. In ista quaestione videtur esse controversia inter philosophos et theologos ; tenent enim philosophi perfectionem naturae, et negant perfectionem supernaturalem ; theologi vero cognoscunt defectum naturae et necessitatem gratiae et perfectionum supernaturalium.

6. Diceret ergo philosophus quod nulla est cognitio supernaturalis homini necessaria pro isto statu, sed quod omnem notitiam sibi necessariam posset acquirere ex actione causarum naturalium. Ad hoc adducitur simul auctoritas et ratio Philosophi ex diversis locis.

(a) Primo per illud II *de anima* ubi dicit quod intellectus agens est quo est omnia facere, et intellectus possibilis est quo est omnia fieri. Ex hoc arguitur sic : activo naturali et passivo debite approximatis et non impeditis necessario sequitur actio, quia non dependet essentialiter nisi ab eis tanquam a causis prioribus ; activum autem respectu omnium intelligibilium est intellectus agens, et passivum

77

est intellectus possibilis, et haec sunt naturaliter in anima, nec sunt simpliciter impedita ; patet ergo quod virtute naturali istorum potest sequi actus intelligendi respectu cuiuscumque intelligibilis. Confirmatur ratio : omni potentiae passivae naturali correspondet aliquod activum naturale, alioquin videretur potentia passiva esse frustra in natura, si per nihil in natura posset reduci ad actum ; sed intellectus possibilis est potentia passiva et naturalis respectu quorumcumque intelligibilium ; ergo correspondet sibi aliqua potentia activa naturalis. Sequitur ergo propositum. Minor patet, quia intellectus possibilis naturaliter appetit cognitionem cuiuscumque cognoscibilis ; naturaliter etiam perficitur per quamcumque cognitionem ; ergo est naturaliter receptivus cuiuscumque intellectionis.

(**b**) Praeterea, vi *Metaphys.*, dividitur scientia speculativa in metaphysicam et physicam sive naturalem et mathematicam. Et ex probatione eius ibidem non videtur possibile plures habitus esse speculativos, quia in istis consideratur de toto ente, et in se et quoad omnes partes eius. Sicut autem non posset esse aliqua alia scientia speculativa ab istis, sic nec practica aliqua alia a practicis acquisitis activis et factivis. Ergo scientiae practicae acquisitae sufficiunt ad perficiendum intellectum practicum, et speculativae acquisitae sufficiunt ad perficiendum intellectum speculativum.

(**c**) Praeterea, potens naturaliter intelligere principium potest naturaliter cognoscere et intelligere conclusiones inclusas in principio. Hanc probo : quia scientia conclusionum non dependet nisi ex intellectu principii et ex deductione conclusionum ex principio, sicut patet ex definitione scire, i *Posteriorum* ; sed deductio est ex se manifesta, sicut patet ex definitione syllogismi perfecti, i *Priorum,* quia nullius est indigens ut appareat evidenter necessarius. Ergo si principia intelliguntur, et deductio manifesta est ex se, habentur omnia quae sunt necessaria ad scientiam conclusionis. Patet ergo maior. Sed naturaliter intelligimus principia prima, in quibus virtualiter includuntur omnes conclusiones scibiles ; ergo naturaliter possumus scire omnes conclusiones istas scibiles. Probatio primae partis minoris : quia termini primorum principiorum sunt communissimi ; ergo istos naturaliter cognoscimus ut possumus naturaliter cognoscere sive intelligere, quia ex I *Physic.* communissima a nobis primo intelliguntur quia sunt sicut ianua in domo, I *Metaphys.* Ergo terminos dictos naturaliter cognoscimus : principia autem cognoscimus in quantum terminos cognoscimus, I *Posteriorum* ; ergo principia prima possumus naturaliter cognoscere. Probatio secundae partis minoris : quia termini primorum principiorum sunt communissimi, ergo quando distribuuntur distribuuntur pro omnibus conceptibus inferioribus : accipiuntur autem tales termini universaliter in primis principiis, et ita extendunt se ad omnes conceptus particulares, et per consequens ad extrema omnium specialium conclusionum. *Quare,* etc.

ARTICULUS II

7. Contra istam positionem potest argui tripliciter. Primo sic : omni agenti per cognitionem necessaria est distincta cognitio sui finis. Hanc probo : quia omne agens propter finem agit ex appetitu finis, et omne per se agens agit propter finem, ergo omne per se agens suo modo appetit finem ; ergo sicut agenti naturali est necessarius appetitus finis propter quem debet agere, ita agenti per cognitionem (quod etiam est per se agens, ex II *Physic.*) necessarius est appetitus sui finis proper quem debet agere qui sequitur cognitionem. Patet ergo maior. Sed homo non potest scire ex naturalibus finem suum distincte ; ergo necessaria est sibi de hoc tradi aliqua cognitio super- naturalis.

(**a**) Minor patet primo : quia philosophus sequens naturalem rationem aut ponit felicitatem esse perfectam in cognitione substantiarum separatarum acquisita, sicut videtur dicere I *Ethic.* et x, aut si non determinate asserit istam esse supremam perfectionem nobis possibilem, aliquam aliam tamen ratione naturali non concludit, ita quod soli rationi naturali innitendo vel errabit circa finem in particulari vel dubius remanebit. Unde I *Ethic.*, C. xiii, dubitando ait : Siquidem igitur et aliud aliquod deorum est donum hominibus, rationabile felicitatem Dei datum esse, et maxime humanorum quantum optimum.

(**b**) Secundo probatur eadem minor per rationem : quia nullius substantiae finis proprius cognoscitur a nobis nisi ex actibus eius nobis manifestis ex quibus ostenditur quod talis finis sit conveniens tali naturae ; nullos autem actus experimur nec cognoscimus inesse naturae nostrae in statu isto ex quibus cognoscamus visionem substantia- rum separatarum esse convenientem nobis ; ergo non possumus naturaliter cognoscere distincte quod iste finis sit conveniens naturae nostrae. Hos saltem certum est, quod quaedam conditiones finis, propter quas est appeti- bilior et ferventius inquirendus, non possunt determinate concludi ratione naturali. Etsi enim daretur quod ratio naturalis sufficeret ad probandum quod visio nuda et fruitio Dei est finis hominis, tamen non concluderetur quod illa perpetuo convenit homini perfecto in corpore et anima, sicut dicetur IV, Dist. xliii. Et tamen perpetuitas huius boni est conditio reddens finem appetibiliorem quam si esset transitorius. Consequi etiam hoc bonum in natura perfecta appetibilius est quam in anima separata, sicut patet per August. XII *super Genesim*. Istas ergo et similes conditiones finis necessarium est noscere ad efficaciter inquirendum finem ; at tamen ad eas non sufficit ratio naturalis. Ergo requiritur doctrina supernaturaliter tradita.

8. Secundo sic : omni cognoscenti agenti propter finem necessaria est triplex cognitio : primo quomodo et qualiter finis acquiratur, secundo cognitio omnium quae sunt necessaria ad finem, tertio est necessarium cognoscere quod omnia ista sufficiant ad talem finem. Primum patet, quia si nesciat quomodo finis acquiratur, nesciet qualiter ad consecutionem illius se disponat. Secundum probatur, quia si nesciat omnia necessaria ad ipsum finem, propter ignorantiam alicuius necessarii poterit a fine deficere. Et etiam quantum ad tertium, si nesciat ista necessaria sufficere, dubitando se ignorare aliquod necessarium, non efficaciter prosequetur illud quod est necessarium. Sed haec tria non potest viator ratione naturali cognoscere. Probatio primi : quia beatitudo confertur tamquam praemium pro meritis eius quem Deus acceptat tanquam dignum tali praemio ; et per consequens nulla naturali necessitate sequitur ad actus nostros qualescumque, sed contingenter datur a Deo actus aliquos in ordine ad ipsam tanquam meritorios acceptante. Hoc autem non est naturaliter scibile, ut videtur, quia in hoc errabant philosophi ponentes omnia quae sunt a Deo immediate esse ab eo necessario. Saltem alia duo membra sunt immanifesta ; non enim potest sciri naturaliter acceptatio voluntatis divinae, ut puta tamquam contingenter acceptantis talia vel talia digna vita aeterna ; et quod etiam illa sufficiant, dependet mere ex voluntate divina circa ea ad quae contingenter se habet ; *ergo*, etc.

9. Contra istas duas rationes instatur ; et primo contra primam sic : (**a**) Omnis natura creata essentialiter dependet a qualibet per se causa ; et propter talem dependentiam ex causato cognito potest demonstratione quia quaelibet eius per se causa cognosci ; ergo cum natura hominis sit homini naturaliter cognoscibilis, quia non est potentiae cognitivae improportionalis, sequitur quod ex ista natura cognita possit naturaliter cognosci finis illius naturae.

(**b**) Confirmatur ratio : quia si ex natura inferiori cognita cognoscitur eius finis, non minus hoc est possibile in proposito, quia nec minor dependentia est finiti in proposito ad suum finem quam in aliis.

(**c**) Ex hac etiam ratione videtur quod falsa sit ista propositio, finis substantiae non cognoscitur nisi ex actibus eius, quae assumebatur in probatione minoris, quia ex cognitione naturae in se potest finis eius cognosci demonstratione quia.

(**d**) Si autem dicatur, quod ratio concludit hominem naturaliter posse cognoscere suum finem naturalem, non autem supernaturalem ; contra, Aug. I *de praedestinatione sanctorum*, C.v. : Proinde inquit, posse habere fidem sicut posse habere charitatem naturae est hominum ; habere autem fidem quemadmodum habere charitatem gratiae est fidelium. Si igitur natura hominis est naturaliter cognoscibilis homini, naturaliter etiam erit cognoscibilis ista potentia ut est talis naturae, et per consequens ordinabilitas talis naturae ad finem ad quem fides et charitas disponit.

(**e**) Item, homo naturaliter appetit finem istum quem dicis supernaturalem ; igitur ad istum naturaliter ordinatur ; ergo ex tali ordine potest concludi iste finis ex cognitione naturae ordinatae ad ipsum.

(**f**) Item, naturaliter cognoscibile est primum obiectum intellectus esse ens, secundum Avic. III *Metaphys.*, et naturaliter est cognoscibile in Deo perfectissime salvari rationem entis ; finis autem cuiuscumque potentiae est optimum eorum quae continentur sub eius obiecto primo, quia in illo solo est perfecta quietatio et delectatio ex x *Ethic.* ; igitur naturaliter cognoscibile est hominem ordinari secundum intellectum ad Deum tamquam ad finem.

(**g**) Confirmatur ratio, quia cui naturaliter est cognoscibilis potentia aliqua, sibi naturaliter est cognoscibile quid sit eius obiectum primum ; et ulterius potest cognoscere in quo perfectissime salvatur ratio illius primi obiecti ; quod tale perfectissimum est finis potentiae ; mens autem nota est sibi, secundum Aug. xiv *de Trinitate*, C. iv ; igitur notum est sibi quid sit eius primum obiectum. Et novit Deum non excludi a ratione illius primi obiecti, quia tunc nullo modo esset ab ipsa mente intelligibilis ; ergo novit Deum esse optimum in quo salvatur ratio sui primi obiecti, et ita novit ipsum esse finem potentiae.

10. Contra secundam rationem arguitur sic : (**a**) si per unum extremum cognoscitur aliud, ergo et medium. Sed necessaria ad consequendum finem sunt media inter naturam et finem suum consequendum ; igitur cum ex cognitione naturae possit cognosci finis naturae, secundum prius probata, videtur quod similiter possint cognosci media necessaria ad finem. (**b**) Confirmatur ratio : ita enim in proposito entium ad finem videtur esse necessaria connexio ad ipsum finem sicut in aliis ; sed propter talem connexionem in aliis ex fine cognoscuntur illa quae sunt ad finem necessaria, sicut per rationem sanitatis concluditur talia et talia requiri ad sanitatem ; *ergo*, etc.

11. Ad primum, licet procedat de fine qui est causa finalis, non de fine attingendo per operationem, quorum finium distinctio dicetur infra, potest tamen ad istud et ad sequens de Augustino et ad tertium de potentia et primo obiecto dici unica responsione, quod omnia accipiunt nostram naturam vel potentiam intellectivam esse nobis cognoscibilem naturaliter ; quod falsum est, sub illa ratione propria et speciali sub qua ad talem finem ordinatur, et sub qua capax est gratiae consummatae, et sub qua habet Deum pro perfectissimo obiecto. Non enim cognoscitur anima nostra a nobis, nec natura nostra pro statu isto nisi sub ratione aliqua generali abstrahibili a sensibilibus, sicut patebit infra, Dist. iii. Et secundum talem rationem generalem non convenit sibi ordinari ad talem finem nec posse capere gratiam nec habere sic Deum pro obiecto.

Tunc ad formam : cum dicitur quod ex ente ad finem cognito potest cognosci finis demonstratione quia, dicendum, quod non est verum nisi cognito illo ente ad finem sub illa propria ratione sub qua habet finem istum. Et tunc minor est falsa. Et cum probatur per proportionalitatem, dico quod licet mens sit eadem sibi, non tamen pro statu isto est proportionalis sibi tamquam obiectum nisi secundum rationes generales quae possunt abstrahi ab imaginabilibus.

Ad confirmationem dico, quod nec aliarum substantiarum fines proprii cognoscuntur, qui scilicet sunt earum secundum rationes proprias, nisi aliqui sint actus manifesti ex quibus concludatur ordo earum ad talem finem.

Et ex hoc patet ad illud quod adducitur contra probationem minoris, quod ista propositio non est falsa : Non cognoscitur a nobis finis proprius substantiae nisi per actus eius nobis manifestos. Non enim accipit propositio illa quod non possit aliter cognosci finis ; bene enim est verum quod si substantia sub propria ratione cognosceretur, ex natura sic cognita posset eius causa per se cognosci demonstratione quia ; sed non sic cognoscitur a nobis aliqua substantia nunc ; ideo nullum finem possumus nunc concludere proprium substantiae nisi per actum evidentem de illa substantia ut sic nota in universali et confuse. In proposito autem deficit utraque via. Sed probatio minoris tetigit unam viam de ignorantia actus supponendo aliam de ignorantia naturae in se.

Ad secundum de Augustino dico, quod illa potentia habendi charitatem, ut ipsa est dispositio respectu Dei in se sub propria ratione amandi, convenit naturae hominis secundum rationem specialem, non communem sibi et sensibilibus, et ideo non est illa potentialitas naturaliter cognoscibilis de homine, sicut nec homo cognoscitur sub illa ratione sub qua est eius haec potentia. Et ita respondeo ad illud, in quantum potest adduci contra conclusionem principalem, scilicet oppositam minori primae rationis. Sed in quantum adducitur contra illam responsionem de fine naturali et supernaturali, concedo Deum esse finem naturalem hominis licet non naturaliter adipiscendum sed supernaturaliter. Et hoc probat ratio sequens de desiderio naturali, quam concedo.

Ad aliud negandum est illud quod assumitur, scilicet quod naturaliter cognoscimus ens esse primum obiectum intellectus nostri, et hoc secundum totam indifferentiam entis ad sensibilia et insensibilia. Et hoc quod dicit Avicenna non concludit quod sit naturaliter notum ; miscuit enim sectam suam, quae fuit secta Mahometi, philosophicis ; et quaedam dixit ut philosophica et ratione probata, alia ut consona suae sectae. Unde ipse expresse ponit libro III *Metaphys.* suae, animam separatam cognoscere substantiam immaterialem in se ; et ideo sub obiecto primo intellectus habet ponere substantiam immaterialem contineri. Non sic Aristoteles, sed secundum ipsum videtur esse primum obiectum intellectus nostri quidditas rei sensibilis, et hoc vel in se sensibilis vel in suo inferiori, hoc est quidditas abstrahibilis a sensibilibus.

Quod autem additur de Augustino in confirmatione illius rationis respondeo et dico, quod dictum Augustini debet intelligi de actu primo sufficiente ex se omnino ad actum suum secundum ; sed tamen nunc impeditur, propter quod impedimentum actus secundus non elicitur a primo. De hoc autem amplius dicetur infra.

Si vero obiiciatur contra ista : homo in statu innocentiae vel naturae institutae potuit cognoscere naturam suam, igitur finem naturae ex deductione primae rationis ; igitur ista cognitio non est supernaturalis. Item contra responsionem ad ultimam rationem : si ideo non cognoscitur quid sit obiectum primum intellectus, quia non cognoscitur intellectus sub ratione propria sub qua respicit tale obiectum, ergo non potest cognosci de quocumque, quod ipsum sit intelligibile, quia non cognoscitur potentia sub illa ratione sub qua respicit quodcumque ut obiectum intelligibile, respondeo ad primum : requireretur dici, qualis fuerit cognitio hominis instituti, quod usque alias differatur ; saltem respectu viatoris pro statu isto est dicta cognitio supernaturalis, quia facultatem eius naturalem excedens ; naturalem dico secundum statum naturae lapsae.

Ad secundum concedo quod non habetur modo cognitio de anima vel de aliqua eius potentia ita distincta, quod ex ipsa possit cognosci quod aliquod obiectum tale intelligibile sibi correspondeat ; sed ex ipso actu quem experimur concludimus potentiam et naturam cuius iste actus est illud respicere pro obiecto quod percipimus attingi per actum : ita quod obiectum potentiae non concluditur ex cognitione potentiae sed ex cognitione actus quem experimur. Sed de obiecto supernaturali neutram cognitionem possumus habere ; ideo ibi deficit utraque via cognoscendi finem proprium illius naturae.

12. Ad argumentum contra secundam rationem patet, quia supponit quoddam iam negatum. Ad confirmationem illius rationis dico, quod quando finis sequitur naturaliter ea quae sunt ad finem et naturaliter praeexigit illa, tunc ex fine possunt concludi ea quae sunt ad finem ; hic autem non est consecutio naturalis sed tantum acceptatio divinae voluntatis compensantis ista merita tamquam digna tali fine et tali praemio.

13. Tertio arguitur principaliter contra opinionem philosophorum, vii *Metaphys.* : cognitio substantiarum separatarum est nobilissima, quia est circa nobilissimum genus ; ergo cognitio eorum quae sunt propria eis est maxime nobilis et necessaria ; nam illa propria eis sunt nobiliora et perfectiora cognoscibilia quam illa in quibus conveniunt cum sensibilibus ; sed illa propria non possumus cognoscere ex puris naturalibus.

Probo (**a**) quia si in aliqua scientia naturaliter possibili traderentur haec propria, hoc esset in metaphysica ; sed ipsa non est possibilis naturaliter a nobis haberi de propriis passionibus istarum substantiarum separatarum, ut patet dupliciter. Et primo sic : quia illa non includuntur virtualiter in primo subiecto metaphysicae, scilicet in ente. Hoc etiam est quod dicit philosophus, i *Metaphys.*, quod oportet sapientem omnia cognoscere aliqualiter, scilicet in universali et non in particulari. Et subdit : qui enim novit universalia novit aliqualiter omnia subiecta ; sapientem autem vocat metaphysicum, sicut metaphysicam probat ibi esse sapientiam.

(**b**) Secundo probo ratione : quia non cognoscuntur talia cognitione propter quid nisi cognoscantur eorum propria subiecta, quae subiecta includunt talia propter quid ; sed propria subiecta eorum non sunt a nobis naturaliter cognoscibilia ; *ergo*, etc. Nec cognoscuntur illa propria eorum demonstratione quia, videlicet ex effectibus. Quod probatur : nam effectus vel relinquunt intellectum dubium quoad ista vel adducunt in errorem. Quod apparet ex proprietatibus Primae Substantiae immaterialis in se ; proprietas enim naturae eius est quod sit communicabilis tribus ; sed effectus non ostendunt istam proprietatem, quia non sunt ab ipso in quantum trinus. Et si ab effectibus arguatur ad causam, magis ducunt in oppositum et in errorem, quia in nullo effectu invenitur una natura numero nisi in uno supposito. Proprietas etiam istius naturae ad extra est causare contingenter ; et ad oppositum huius magis deducunt effectus in errorem, sicut patet per opiniones philosophorum ponentium Primum necessario causare. De proprietatibus etiam aliarum substantiarum patet hoc idem, quia effectus magis ducunt in sempiternitatem et aeternitatem et necessitatem earum quam in contingentiam et novitatem. Similiter videntur philosophi ex motibus concludere quod numerus istarum substantiarum separatarum sit secundum numerum motuum coelestium. Similiter quod illae substantiae sunt naturaliter beatae et impeccabiles, sicut philosophi posuerunt. Quae omnia absurdissima sunt.

14. Contra istam rationem arguo et probo quod quaecumque necessaria de substantiis separatis cognoscuntur a nobis nunc per fidem sive per communem vel specialem revelationem possunt cognosci cognitione naturali. Et hoc sic : quorumcumque necessariorum revelatorum terminos naturaliter cognoscimus, et illa possumus naturaliter comprehendere ; sed omnium necessariorum revelatorum terminos naturaliter cognoscimus ; *ergo*, etc. Probatio maioris : illa necessaria aut sunt mediata aut immediata. Si immediata, ergo cognoscuntur cognitis terminis, I *Posteriorum.* Si mediata, ergo cum possumus cognoscere extrema, possumus concipere medium inter ea ; et tunc coniungendo illud medium cum utroque extremo aut habentur praemissae mediate aut immediate. Si immediate, idem quod prius. Si mediate, procedemus concipiendo medium inter extrema, et coniungendo cum extremis quousque veniamus ad immediata. Igitur

tandem veniemus ad necessaria immediata quae intelligemus ex terminis ex quibus sequuntur omnia necessaria mediata ; ergo ista mediata per immediata scire poterimus naturaliter. Probatio minoris principalis : quia habens fidem et non habens fidem contradicentes sibi invicem non contendunt de nominibus tantum sed de conceptibus : sicut cum philosophus et theologus contradicunt de ista, Deus est trinus et unus, ubi non tantum idem nomen sed eundem conceptum unus negat et alius affirmat ; ergo omnem conceptum simplicem quem iste habet et ille habet.

15. Ad istud respondeo : de substantiis separatis sunt aliquae veritates immediatae. Accipio tunc aliquam veritatem talem primam et immediatam, et sit A. In ista includuntur multae veritates mediatae, puta omnes quae particulariter enunciant communia ad praedicatum de communibus ad subiectum ; dicantur B, C. Ista vera mediata non habent evidentiam nisi ex aliquo immediato ; ergo non sunt nata sciri nisi ex isto immediato intellecto. Si igitur aliquis intellectus possit immediate intelligere terminos B, C, et componere eos ad invicem, non autem posset intelligere terminos A, nec per consequens ipsum A, B et C erunt intellectui suo propositio neutra. Ita est de nobis, quia conceptus quosdam communes habemus de substantiis immaterialibus et materialibus, et istos possumus ad invicem componere. Sed istae complexiones non habent evidentiam nisi ex veris immediatis, quae sunt de illis quidditatibus sub ratione propria et speciali, sub qua ratione non concipimus istas quidditates, et ideo nec scimus illas veritates generales de conceptibus generalibus.

Exemplum : si impossibile est alicui concipere triangulum sub propria ratione, potest tamen abstrahere rationem figurae a quadrangulo et eam concipere, impossibile est etiam sibi concipere primitatem ut est propria passio trianguli, quia sic non concipitur nisi ut abstrahitur a triangulo ; tamen potest primitatem abstrahere ab aliis primitatibus, puta in numeris. Iste intellectus licet posset formare hanc complexionem, aliqua figura est prima, quia terminos eius potest apprehendere, tamen illa compositio formata erit sibi neutra, quia ista est mediata inclusa in ista immediata, triangulus est sic primus, et hanc immediatam non potest intelligere, quia nec terminos eius ; ideo mediatam non potest scire, quae ex hac immediata tantum habet evidentiam.

Per hoc ad argumentum nego maiorem. Ad probationem dico quod illa necessaria sunt mediata. Et cum dicis : igitur cum possumus cognoscere extrema possumus concipere medium inter extrema, nego consequentiam ; quia medium inter extrema quandoque est essentialiter ordinatum, puta, quod quid est alterius extremi vel passio prior respectu posterioris passionis ; et tale est medium ad concludendum universaliter extremum de extremo. Concedo igitur quod quicumque intellectus potest intelligere extrema potest intelligere tale medium inter talia extrema, quia intellectus eius includitur in altero extremo vel est idem alteri. Si autem medium sit particulare contentum sub altero extremo et non essentialiter ordinatum inter extrema, tunc non oportet quod potens concipere extrema generalia possit concipere medium particulare ad illa extrema generalia. Ita est hic, nam ista quidditas sub ratione propria et particulari, habens passionem aliquam sibi immediate inhaerentem, est medium inferius ad conceptum sibi communem de quo dicitur illa passio in communi accepta, et ideo non est medium essentiale vel universaliter inferens passionem de communi sed tantum particulariter. Hoc patet in exemplo illo, quia non oportet quod potens concipere figuram in communi et primitatem in communi possit concipere triangulum in particulari, quia triangulus est medium contentum sub figura, medium, inquam, ad concludendum primitatem particulariter de figura.

Haec ratio tertia quae adducta est contra opinionem philosophorum potissime concludit de Prima Substantia immateriali, quia eius tamquam obiecti beatifici potissimum est cognitio necessaria nobis. Et tunc responsio ista ad obiectionem contra ipsam supponit unum : quod naturaliter in se non concipimus Deum nisi in conceptu generali communi sibi et sensibilibus, quod inferius Dist. iii, q. I, exponetur. Si etiam negetur illud suppositum, adhuc oporteret dicere, conceptum qui potest fieri de Deo virtute creaturae esse imperfectum ; qui autem fieret respectu Dei et virtute ipsius essentiae esse perfectum. Sicut ergo dictum est de conceptu generali et speciali, ita dicatur secundum aliam viam de imperfecto et perfecto conceptu.

16. Quarto principaliter arguitur sic : ordinatum ad aliquem finem, ad quem est ex se indispositum, necesse est paulatim promoveri ad dispositionem respectu illius finis ; sed homo ordinatur ad finem supernaturalem, ad quem ex se est indispositus ; ergo indiget paulatim disponi ad habendum illum finem ; hoc autem fit per cognitionem aliquam supernaturalem ; *ergo*, etc. Si instetur quod agens perfectum potest statim removere imperfectionem et statim agere, respondetur, quod si posset de potentia absoluta, tamen perfectius est communicare homini activitatem respectu suae perfectionis consequendae quam non communicare ; potest autem homo habere activitatem aliquam respectu suae perfectionis finalis ; ergo perfectius est quod hoc sibi communicetur, quod non potest fieri sine aliqua cognitione imperfecta praecedente istam perfectam, ad quam ordinatur finaliter.

17. Quinto arguitur sic : omne agens utens instrumento in agendo non potest per illud instrumentum in aliquam actionem quae excedit naturam illius instrumenti;

lumen autem intellectus agentis est instrumentum quo anima nunc utitur in intelligendo naturaliter ; ergo non potest per illud lumen in aliquam actionem quae excedit illud lumen ; sed illud de se est limitatum ad cognitionem habitam per viam sensuum ; ergo anima non potest in aliquam cognitionem quae non potest haberi per viam sensus ; sed multorum aliorum cognitio est necessaria pro statu isto nobis quae non possunt haberi per viam sensus ; *igitur*, etc.

Haec ratio videtur concludere contra eum qui fecit eam ; secundum enim deductionem istam lux increata non poterit uti intellectu agente ut instrumento ad cognitionem alicuius sincerae veritatis ; quia talis secundum eum non potest haberi via sensuum sine speciali illustratione. Et ita sequitur quod in cognitione veritatis sincerae lumen intellectus agentis nullo modo habeat aliquam actionem. Quod videtur inconveniens, quia ista actio perfectior est communi omni intellectione, et per consequens illud quod perfectius est in anima in quantum intellectiva oportet concurrere aliquo modo in istam actionem.

Istae duae rationes non videntur plurimum efficaces : prima enim esset efficax si esset probatum quod homo ordinatur finaliter ad cognitionem supernaturalem, cuius probatio pertinet ad quaestiones de beatitudine, et si cum hoc ostenderetur cognitionem naturalem non sufficienter disponere pro statu isto ad cognitionem supernaturalem consequendam. Secunda ratio petit duo, scilicet, aliquorum cognitionem esse necessariam quae non possunt cognosci per viam sensuum, et quod lumen intellectus agentis est ad talia cognoscibilia limitatum. Tres ergo primae rationes probabiliores apparent.

ARTICULUS III

18. Ad quaestionem igitur respondeo distinguendo primo qualiter aliquid dicitur supernaturale. Potentia enim receptiva comparatur ad actum quem recipit vel ad agens a quo recipit. Primo modo ipsa est potentia naturalis vel violenta vel neutra. Dicitur naturalis si naturaliter inclinetur ; violenta si sit contra inclinationem naturalem ; neutra si neque inclinatur ad istam formam quam recipit neque ad oppositam. In hac autem comparatione nulla est supernaturalitas. Sed comparando receptivum ad agens a quo recipit formam est naturalitas quando receptivum comparatur ad tale agens quod natum est naturaliter imprimere talem formam in tali passo ; supernaturalitas autem quando comparatur ad tale agens quod non est naturaliter impressivum illius formae in illud passum.

19. Ad propositum dico quod comparando intellectum possibilem ad notitiam actualem in se nulla est sibi cognitio supernaturalis, quia intellectus possibilis quacumque cognitione naturaliter perficitur et ad quamcumque naturaliter inclinatur. Sed secundo modo loquendo sic est supernaturalis quia generatur ab aliquo agente quod non est natum movere intellectum possibilem ad talem cognitionem naturaliter. Pro statu autem isto secundum philosophum intellectus possibilis natus est moveri ad cognitionem ab intellectu agente .et phantasmate ; igitur sola illa cognitio naturalis est quae ab istis agentibus potest imprimi. Virtute autem istorum potest haberi omnis cognitio incomplexa quae secundum legem communem habetur a viatore, sicut patet in instantia contra tertiam rationem principalem. Et ideo licet Deus possit per revelationem specialem cognitionem alicuius incomplexi causare, sicut in raptu, non tamen talis cognitio supernaturalis est necessaria de communi lege. De complexis

93

autem veritatibus secus est, quia, sicut ostensum est per tres rationes primas contra primam opinionem adductas, posita tota actione intellectus agentis et phantasmatum, multae complexiones remanebunt ignotae et nobis neutrae, quarum cognitio est nobis necessaria. Istarum igitur notitiam est necesse nobis supernaturaliter tradi quia nullus earum notitiam potuit naturaliter invenire et eam aliis docendo tradere, quia sicut uni ita cuilibet ex naturalibus erunt neutrae. Utrum autem post primam traditionem doctrinae de talibus possit aliquis assentire naturaliter doctrinae traditae, de hoc in III lib., Dist. xxiii.

20. Haec autem prima traditio talis doctrinae dicitur revelatio, quae ideo est supernaturalis quia est ab agente quod non est naturaliter motivum intellectus nostri pro statu isto. Aliter etiam posset dici supernaturalis quia est ab agente supplente vicem obiecti supernaturalis. Nam obiectum natum causare notitiam huius, Deus est trinus et unus, vel similium est essentia sub propria ratione cognita ; ipsa autem sub tali ratione cognoscibilis est obiectum nobis supernaturale. Quodcumque igitur agens causat notitiam aliquarum veritatum, quae per tale obiectum sic cognitum natae sunt esse evidentes, illud agens in hoc supplet vicem illius obiecti. Quod si ipsum agens causaret notitiam perfectam istarum veritatum qualem ipsum obiectum in se cognitum causaret, tunc perfecte suppleret vicem obiecti ; sed si agens non ita perfectam notitiam causat sicut obiectum in se causaret, tunc imperfecte supplet vicem obiecti, pro quanto scilicet imperfecta notitia quam facit virtualiter continetur in illa perfecta cuius obiectum in se cognitum esset causa. Ita in proposito : nam revelans hanc, Deus est trinus, causat in intellectu aliqualem notitiam huius veritatis licet obscuram, quia causat de obiecto non sub propria ratione cognito ; quod obiectum si cognitum esset, natum esset causare notitiam perfectam et claram veritatis illius. Pro quanto igitur haec notitia obscura in illa clara includitur eminenter sicut imperfectum in perfecto, pro tanto revelans hanc obscuram et causans supplet vicem obiecti illius clarae notitiae causativi ; praecipue cum non possit notitiam alicuius veritatis causare nisi ut supplens vicem alicuius obiecti, nec veritatum talium de illo obiecto causare posset ut supplens vicem obiecti alicuius inferioris naturaliter motivi intellectus nostri, et quia nullum tale virtualiter includit aliquam notitiam istarum veritatum, etiam nec obscuram ; igitur oportet quod in causando etiam istam obscuram aliqualiter suppleat vicem obiecti supernaturalis.

Differentia autem istorum duorum modorum ponendi supernaturalitatem notitiae revelatae patet separando unum ab alio : puta, si agens supernaturale causaret notitiam obiecti naturalis, ut si infunderet geometriam alicui, illa esset supernaturalis primo modo et non secundo modo ; si autem infunderet notitiam huius, Deus est trinus, vel similium, haec supernaturalis esset utroque modo, quia secundus infert primum, licet non e converso ; ubi autem est primus tantum, ibi non est necesse quod sit sic supernaturalis, quin naturaliter possit haberi ; ubi vero est secundus modus est necessitas ut supernaturaliter habeatur, quia naturaliter haberi non potest.

ARTICULUS IV

21. Tres rationes primae quibus innititur ista solutio confirmantur per auctoritates. (**a**) Primo per auctoritatem August. *de civitate Dei* lib. xviii, C. xli iuxta finem, ubi ait : Philosophi, inquit, nescientes ad quem finem referenda ista essent, inter falsa quae locuti sunt, verum videre potuerunt.

(**b**) Secunda ratio confirmatur per August. xi *de civitate Dei*, C. ii : quid prodest nosse quo eundum sit, si ignoratur via qua eundum sit ? In hoc enim errabant philosophi, quia etsi aliqua de virtutibus vera tradiderunt, tamen falsa miscuerunt, secundum auctoritatem praecedentem Aug., et patet ex eorum libris. Improbat enim Aristoteles politias dispositas a multis aliis, ii *Politicorum* ; sed nec illa Aristotelis est irreprehensibilis, xii *Politicorum,* ubi docet deos esse honorandos : Decet, inquit, cultum exhibere diis ; et ibidem C. v : Lex nullum orbatum tradit nutriri ; et in eodem lib. C. viii dicit quod oportet fieri aborsum in casu.

(**c**) Tertia ratio confirmatur per Aug. xi *de civitate Dei,* C. iii : quae remota sunt a sensibus nostris, quae testimonio nostro scire non possumus, de his alios testes requirimus. Et hoc confirmat totam solutionem principalem, quia enim veritates illae de quibus argutum est nobis ipsae ex se sunt neutrae, nullus potest suo testimonio credere de ipsis, sed oportet testimonium supernaturale requirere alicuius superioris tota specie humana.

(**d**) Qualiter autem prima revelatio sive traditio talis doctrinae fieri potuerit et facta sit, est dubium an scilicet locutione interiore an exteriore an cum aliquibus signis adhibitis sufficientibus ad causandum assensum. Ad propositum sufficit quod utroque modo potuit supernaturaliter revelari talis doctrina. Sed neutro modo potuit ab homine sine errore primo tradi.

22. Contra istas tres rationes instatur simul quod se ipsas destruant : quia quod ostenditur esse necessario cognoscendum, hoc ostenditur esse verum, quia nihil scitur nisi verum ; ergo quidquid istae rationes ostendunt intellectui esse necessarium cognosci : puta quod fruitio Dei in se sit finis hominis, quoad primam rationem, quod via deveniendi ad ipsam est per merita, quae Deus acceptat ut digna tali praemio quoad secundum, quod Deus est trinus et contingenter causans et huiusmodi quoad tertiam ; totum illud ostenditur esse verum. Vel ergo illae rationes non sunt nisi ex fide, vel ex ipsis concluditur oppositum eius quod probant. (**b**) Respondeo : naturali ratione ostenditur necessarium esse scire alteram partem determinate huius contradictionis : fruitio est finis : fruitio non est finis ; hoc est, quod intellectus non sit mere dubius vel neuter in hoc problemate, an fruitio sit finis, quia talis dubitatio vel ignorantia impediret inquisitionem finis. Non autem ostenditur ratione naturali quod haec pars sit necessario cognoscenda. Et hoc modo rationes praedictae ut sunt naturales concludunt de altera parte contradictionis, hac vel illa, non determinate de hac nisi ex creditis tantum.

ARTICULUS V

23. Ad argumenta pro opinione Aristotelis. Ad primum dico quod cognitio dependet ab anima cognoscente et obiecto cognito, quia secundum August. ix *de Trinitate*, C. ult., a cognoscente et cognito paritur notitia. Licet ergo anima habeat sufficiens activum et passivum intra se pro quanto actio respectu cognitionis convenit animae, non tamen habet intra se sufficiens activum pro quanto actio convenit obiecto, quia sic est ut tabula nuda, ut dicitur *de anima*. Est igitur intellectus agens quo est omnia facere : verum est in quantum factio sive actio competit animae respectu cognitionis, et non in quantum obiectum est activum.

Ad confirmationem rationis dico ad maiorem quod natura quandoque accipitur pro principio intrinseco motus vel quietis prout describitur ii *Physicorum* : quandoque pro principio activo naturali, prout natura distinguitur contra artem sive propositum propter oppositum modum princi-

piandi. Primo modo non est vera maior, quia non correspondet omni passivo naturali principium activum quod
sic sit natura, quia multa sunt naturaliter receptiva alicuius
perfectionis cuius non habent principium intrinsecum
activum. Secundo modo etiam propositio maior est falsa
in quibusdam, quando scilicet natura propter sui excel-
lentiam ordinatur naturaliter ad recipiendum perfectionem
ita eminentem ,quod non possit subesse causalitati agentis
naturalis secundo modo dicti, et ita est in proposito. Cum
probatur maior, dico quod potentia passiva non est
frustra in natura ; quia licet per agens naturale non possit
principaliter reduci ad actum, tamen potest per tale agens
dispositio ad ipsum induci, et potest per aliquod aliud
agens in natura, id est in tota coordinatione entium, puta
per agens supernaturale, complete reduci ad actum.

Si autem obiiciatur quod illud vilificat naturam, quod
ipsa non possit consequi perfectionem suam ex naturalibus,
cum natura minus deficiat in nobilioribus, ex II *coeli et
mundi,* respondeo : si felicitas nostra consisteret in specu-
latione illa suprema ad quam possumus nunc naturaliter
attingere, non diceret philosophus naturam deficere in
necessariis ; nunc autem concedo illam posse naturaliter haberi ; et ultra hoc dico aliam eminentiorem posse naturaliter recipi ; ergo in hoc magis dignificatur natura quam si
suprema sibi possibilis poneretur solum esse illa naturalis.
Nec mirum quod ad maiorem perfectionem sit capacitas
passiva in aliqua natura quam eius causalitas activa se
extendat. Illud autem quod additur de II *coeli et mundi* non
est ad propositum, quia philosophus loquitur ibidem de
organis correspondentibus potentiae motivae, si ipsa
inesset stellis, quod natura dedisset eis organa ; et concedo
universaliter, quod cui datur potentia quae nata est esse
organica, et datur a natura organum, in non orbatis dico.
Sed in proposito dico quod data est potentia sed non

organica ; non tamen sunt naturaliter data omnia alia praeter potentiam concurrentia ad actum. A philosopho igitur ibi haberi potest quod naturaliter ordinabile ad aliquem actum vel obiectum naturaliter habet potentiam ad illud et organum requisitum ad actum, si potentia est organica ; sed non sic de posterioribus requisitis ad actum.

Aliter tamen posset dici ad maiorem, quod ipsa est vera loquendo de potentia passiva naturali ut passiva comparatur ad activam, non autem ut passiva comparatur ad actum receptum. Differentia membrorum patet in principio solutionis istius quaestionis. Minor vero est vera secundo modo, non primo.

Posset autem tertio modo facilius dici ad minorem negando quod licet absolute intellectus possibilis sit naturaliter receptivus talis intellectionis, non tamen pro statu isto, causa cuius dicetur inferius, distinctione tertia.

24. (**a**) Ad secundum dicitur quod diversa ratio scibilis diversitatem scientiarum inducit ; eamdem enim conclusionem demonstrat astrologus et naturalis, puta, quod terra est rotunda ; sed astrologus per medium mathematicum, id est a materia abstractum, naturalis autem per medium circa materiam consideratum. Unde nihil prohibet de eisdem rebus, de quibus philosophicae scientiae tractant, secundum quod sunt cognoscibilia lumine naturalis rationis, etiam aliam scientiam tractare, secundum quod cognoscuntur lumine divinae revelationis. Contra hoc : si de cognoscibilibus in theologia est cognitio tradita vel possibilis tradi in aliis scientiis, licet in alio lumine, ergo non est de eis necessaria cognitio theologica. Consequentia patet in exemplo eius, quia per medium physicum cognoscens terram esse rotundam non indiget cognitione eius per medium mathematicum tamquam simpliciter necessarium.

Dicta autem responsio ad secundum exponitur sic, quod scilicet habitus et est habitus, et est forma ; in quantum est habitus habet distinctionem ab obiecto, sed in quantum est forma potest distingui a principio activo ; respectu autem habitus scientifici principia sunt causae effectivae. Licet igitur ubi est idem scibile, puta quod terra est rotunda, non sit distinctio per obiecta, tamen est ibi distinctio per principia quibus mathematicus et physicus hoc ostendunt ; et ita est distinctio habituum in quantum sunt formae, et non in quantum sunt habitus.

Contra istud : forma est communis ad habitum, quia omnis habitus est forma, et non e converso ; impossibile est autem aliqua esse distincta in ratione superioris et non esse distincta in ratione inferioris ; ergo impossibile est aliqua esse distincta in ratione formae, et tamen esse indistincta in ratione habituum ; hoc enim esset ac si aliqua essent distincta in ratione animalis et indistincta in ratione hominis. Praeterea, supponit quod principia sunt distinctiva habitus conclusionis in alio genere causae quam ut principia effectiva ; quod falsum est, quia si aliquam rationem causae distinctivae habent ad habitus istos, non habent nisi rationem causae effectivae. Praeterea, semper stat ratio ; quia quantumcumque possent poni habitus cognoscitivi distincti, non tamen salvatur necessitas unius habitus, quasi alia cognitio sit impossibilis, ponendo possibilitatem alterius habitus undecumque distincti.

(**b**) Ideo ad argumentum respondeo quod in illis scientiis speculativis, etsi tractetur de omnibus speculabilibus, non tamen quantum ad omnia cognoscibilia de eis, quia non quantum ad propria eorum cognoscibilia, sicut patuit prius in tertia ratione principali contra opinionem philosophorum.

25. (**a**) Ad tertium respondetur sic : quod prima principia non possunt applicari ad conclusiones aliquas nisi sensibiles ; tum quia termini eorum sunt abstracti a sensibilibus, et ita sapiunt naturam eorum ; tum quia intellectus agens, per quem debet fieri applicatio, limitatur ad sensibilia. Contra, certum est intellectui quod illa principia prima sunt vera non tantum in sensibilibus sed in insensibilibus ; non enim magis dubitatur quod contradictoria non sunt simul vera de eodem immateriali quam materiali ; quare responsio nulla.

(**b**) Et ideo aliter dicitur, quod terminus primi principii est ens quod dividitur in decem genera, et illud non extendit se ad obiectum theologicum. Hoc nihil valet, quia non magis dubitamus quod contradictoria non sunt simul vera de Deo quam de altero, ut quod Deus est beatus et non beatus, verus et non verus quam de albo.

(**c**) Alia datur responsio, quod ex maioribus solum non sequuntur conclusiones sed cum minoribus adiunctis ; nunc autem minores non sunt naturaliter manifestae quae debent illis adiungi. Contra, minores sumendae sub primis principiis praedicant de sumptis sub terminos subiectos primorum principiorum, sed notum est terminos primorum principiorum dici de quolibet quia sunt communissimi ; *ergo. . . .*

(**d**) Ideo respondeo, quod secunda pars minoris est falsa, haec scilicet, quod in primis principiis includuntur virtualiter omnes conclusiones scibiles. Ad probationem dico, quod sicut termini subiecti sunt communes, ita et termini praedicati ; quando igitur termini subiecti sic distributi accipiuntur pro omnibus, non accipiuntur nisi respectu terminorum praedicatorum qui sunt communissimi, et per consequens virtute talium principiorum non sciuntur de inferioribus nisi praedicata communissima. Hoc patet ratione : quia medium non potest esse propter quid respectu alicuius passionis nisi illa passio includitur virtualiter in ratione illius medii ; in ratione autem subiecti principii communissimi non includitur propter quid aliqua passio particularis sed tantum passio communissima ; idem subiectum non potest esse medium vel ratio cognoscendi alia nisi sub illa ratione communissima, et per consequens non est ratio cognoscendi nisi passiones communissimas, sed praeter passiones communissimas sunt multae aliae passiones scibiles, ad quas non possunt rationes primorum terminorum principiorum esse media, quia non includunt illas ; ergo sunt multae veritates scibiles quae non includuntur in primis principiis. Hoc patet ex hoc exemplo : quia istud, omne totum est maius sua parte, etsi includat istam, quaternarius est maior binario, et alias similes de eodem praedicato, non tamen includit istas, scilicet : quaternarius est duplus ad binarium, et ternarius se habet in proportione sexquialtera ad dualitatem ; nam ad ista praedicata oportet habere media specialia concludentia ipsa. Tertia probatio logica est : quia licet contingat descendere sub subiecto universalis affirmativae, non tamen sub praedicato ; multa autem praedicata contenta sub praedicatis primorum principiorum sunt scibilia de inferioribus ad subiecta illorum ; igitur illa praedicata per prima principia non sciuntur de illis subiectis.

Contra istud obiicitur : de quolibet affirmatio vel negatio est de necessitate vera et de nullo obiecto simul ; sequitur ergo de necessitate hoc esse album vel non album, ita quod licet ibi descendere sub praedicato et sub subiecto. Respondeo : illud principium, de quolibet affirmatio vel negatio etc., valet istam : de quolibet cuiuslibet contradictionis altera pars est vera, altera falsa ; ubi duplex est distributio ex parte subiecti, scilicet de quolibet et cuiuslibet, et sub utroque distributo licet descendere ; igitur de hoc huius contradictionis altera pars est vera, altera falsa. Sed sub praedicato confuse tantum non licet descendere, quia non sequitur : de quolibet cuiuslibet altera pars etc., ergo haec pars ; et ita in aliis principiis semper praedicatum universalis affirmativae stat confuse tantum, sive sint ibi duae distributiones in subiecto sive una. Et in proposito exemplo adhuc patet propositum, quia de homine scibile verum est quod sit risibilis, nunquam tamen per hoc principium : de quolibet etc. de homine vero potest plus inferri nisi risibile vel non risibile. Altera igitur pars praedicati disiuncti nunquam scietur de subiecto per hoc principium, sed requiritur aliquod principium speciale de homine.

26. (**a**) Ad argumenta principalia : ad primum distinguo de obiecto naturali, quod potest accipi vel pro eo ad quod naturaliter sive ex actione causarum naturaliter activarum potest potentia attingere vel pro illo ad quod potentia naturaliter inclinatur, sive possit illud naturaliter attingere sive non. Posset ergo maior negari intelligendo obiectum naturale primo modo, quia obiectum primum est adaequatum potentiae et ideo abstractum ab omnibus illis circa quae potest potentia operari ; non autem oportet, si intellectus possit naturaliter intelligere tale commune, quod possit intelligere quodcumque contentum sub illo, quia intellectio alicuius contenti multo excellentior est intellectione confusa talis communis. Et sic, concessa minore in utroque sensu, conclusio intenta non habetur, scilicet de naturaliter attingibili, quia sic maior fuit falsa.

Contra hanc responsionem arguo, quia destruit seipsam. Primum enim obiectum est adaequatum potentiae etiam per ipsum, et verum est, hoc est, quod nihil respicit potentia pro obiecto nisi in quo est ratio illius primi, et in quocumque est ratio illius primi illud respicit potentia pro obiecto ; ergo impossibile est aliquid esse obiectum primum naturaliter, quin quodlibet contentum sub illo sit per se obiectum naturaliter ; da enim oppositum, et tunc non est adaequatum universaliter sive naturaliter sed excedens, et aliquid eo inferius est adaequatum, et ita primum. Ratio autem quae adducitur pro responsione fallit secundum fallaciam figurae dictionis ; licet enim ens, ut est quoddam intelligibile uno actu, sicut homo est intelligibilis una intellectione, sit naturaliter attingibile, illa enim unica intellectio entis ut unius obiecti est naturalis, non tamen ens ut primum obiectum, id est adaequatum, potest poni primum obiectum naturaliter attingibile, nisi quodlibet sub eo contentum sit naturaliter attingibile, quia est primum obiectum ut includitur in omnibus per se obiectis. Commutatur igitur hoc aliquid in quale aliquid cum arguit : ens est naturaliter attingibile ; ergo ens ut primum obiectum, hoc est adaequatum, est naturaliter attingibile ; quia antecedens est verum ut ens est unum intelligibile singulare sicut album ; sed consequens concludit de ente ut includitur in omni intelligibili, non ut seorsum ab aliis intellectum.

(**b**) Ad argumentum igitur est alia responsio realis : quod minor est falsa de obiecto naturali, id est naturaliter attingibili ; vera alio modo de obiecto ad quod naturaliter inclinatur potentia ; et ita debet intelligi auctoritas Avicennae. Quid autem sit ponendum obiectum primum naturaliter attingibile, de hoc infra Dist. iii. Confirmatur responsio per Ansel. *de lib. arbit.*, C. ii : Nullam, inquit, ut puto, habemus potestatem quae sola sufficiat ad actum. Potestatem autem vocat quod nos communiter dicimus potentiam, sicut patet per exemplum eius de sensu visus. Non est igitur inconveniens potentiam esse naturaliter ordinatam ad obiectum ad quod non potest naturaliter ex causis naturalibus attingere, sicut quaelibet ex se sola ordinatur ad actum, et tamen non potest ex se sola attingere.

27. Ad secundum argumentum nego consequentiam. Ad probationem patet ex dictis in responsione ad confirmationem primi argumenti pro opinione philosophi, quod superiora ordinantur ad perfectionem maiorem passive recipiendam quam ipsa possint active producere, et per consequens istorum perfectio non potest produci nisi ab aliquo agente supernaturali ; non sic est de perfectione inferiorum, quorum perfectio ultima potest subesse actioni agentium inferiorum.

28. Ad tertium dico, quod veritati complexae alicui firmiter tenendae intellectus possibilis est improportionatus, hoc est, non est proportionatum mobile respectu talium agentium quae ex phantasmatibus et ex lumine naturali intellectus agentis non possunt cognosci. Cum autem arguis : igitur fit proportionatus per aliquid aliud, concedo ; et per aliud in ratione moventis, quia per movens supernaturale revelans assentit illi veritati ; et per aliud in ratione formae, quia per istum assensum factum in ipso, qui est quasi quaedam inclinatio in intellectu ad illud obiectum proportionans illud isti. Cum ultra de illo alio quaeris, an sit naturale vel supernaturale, dico quod supernaturale, sive intelligas de agente sive de forma. Cum infers ; ergo intellectus est improportionatus ad illud, et per aliud proportionatur, dico quod ex se est in potentia obedientiali ad agens, et ita sufficienter proportionatur illi ad hoc ut ab ipse moveatur. Similiter ex se est capax illius assensus causati a tali agente, et est naturaliter capax. Non oportet ergo ipsum per aliud proportionari illi assensui in recipiendo. Statur igitur in secundo, non in primo, quia veritas ista revelata non est sufficienter inclinativa intellectus ad assentiendum sibi, et ita est improportionale agens, et passum sibi improportionale. Sed agens supernaturale est sufficienter inclinativum intellectus ad istam veritatem causando in ipso assensum quo proportionatur huic veritati, ita quod non oportet intellectum per aliud proportionari tali agente, nec formae ab ipso impressae, sicut oportet ipsum proportionari tali obiecto per aliud duplici modo praedicto.

PRINTED IN GREAT BRITAIN AT
THE PRESS OF THE PUBLISHERS